A-Z MAIDSTONE MEDWAY

CONTENTS

REFERENCE

Motorway	**M20**
A Road	A2
B Road	B2097
Dual Carriageway	
One-way Street	
Traffic flow on A Roads is also indicated by a heavy line on the driver's left.	
Road Under Construction	
Opening dates are correct at the time of publication.	
Proposed Road	
Restricted Access	
Pedestrianized Road	
Track & Footpath	
Residential Walkway	
Railway	Level Crossing / Station / Tunnel / Heritage Station
Built-up Area	QUEEN ST.
Local Authority Boundary	
Posttown Boundary	
Postcode Boundary (within Posttown)	
Map Continuation	10 — Large Scale Town Centre 5
Car Park (selected)	P
Church or Chapel	†

City Wall (large scale only)	
Cycleway (selected)	
Fire Station	■
Hospital	(H)
House Numbers (A & B Roads only)	145 98
Information Centre	i
National Grid Reference	575
Park & Ride	Willington Street P+R
Police Station	▲
Post Office	★
Safety Camera with Speed Limit	(30) fixed speed
Fixed cameras and long term road works cameras Symbols do not indicate camera direction	(V) variable speed
Toilet:	
without facilities for the Disabled	▽
with facilities for the Disabled	▽
Disabled use only	▽
Viewpoint	
Educational Establishment	
Hospital or Healthcare Building	
Industrial Building	
Leisure or Recreational Facility	
Place of Interest	
Public Building	
Shopping Centre & Market	
Other Selected Buildings	

SCALE

Map Page 8-53 1:19,000	Map Page 4-7 1:9,500
3⅓ inches (8.47cm) to 1 mile 5.26cm to 1 km	6⅔ inches (16.94cm) to 1 mile 10.52cm to 1 km
0 — ¼ — ½ Mile	0 — ⅛ — ¼ Mile
0 250 500 750 Metres	0 100 200 300 Metres

Copyright of Geographers' A-Z Map Company Limited

Fairfield Road, Borough Green, Sevenoaks, Kent TN15 8PP
Telephone: 01732 781000 (Enquiries & Trade Sales)
01732 783422 (Retail Sales)
www.az.co.uk
Copyright © Geographers' A-Z Map Co. Ltd.
Edition 7 2013

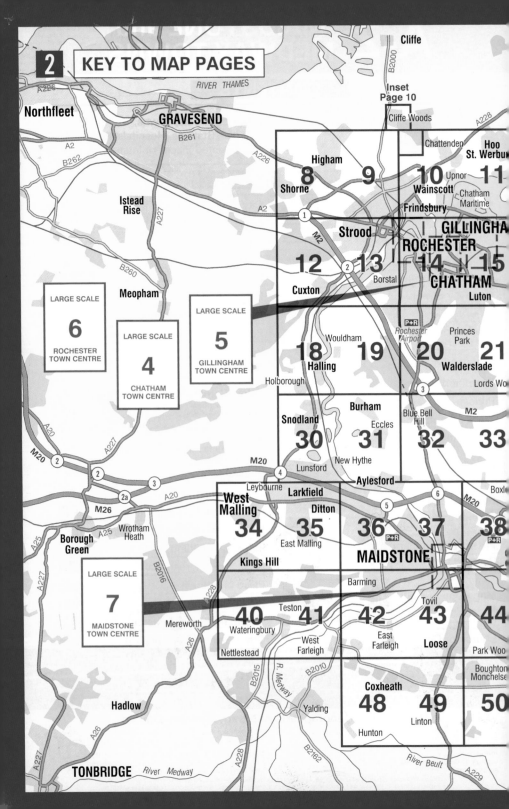

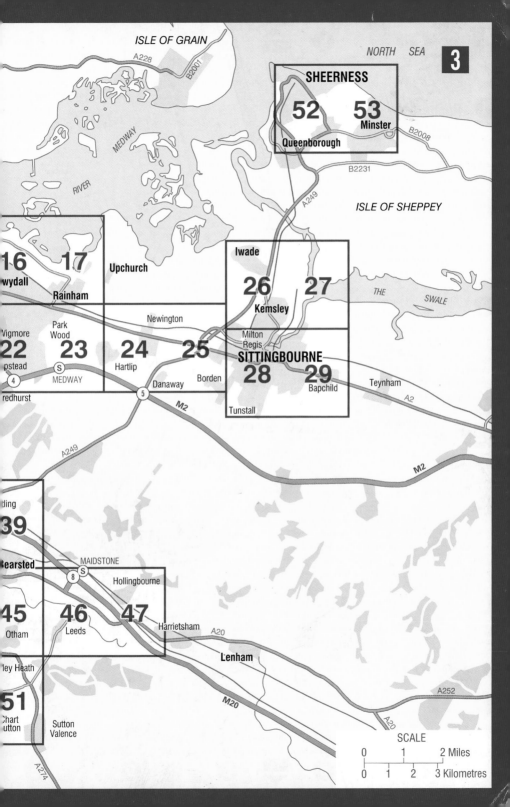

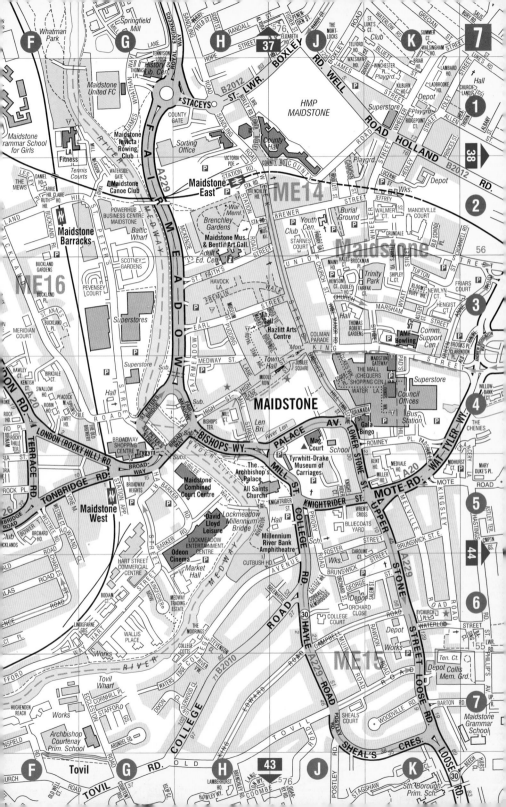

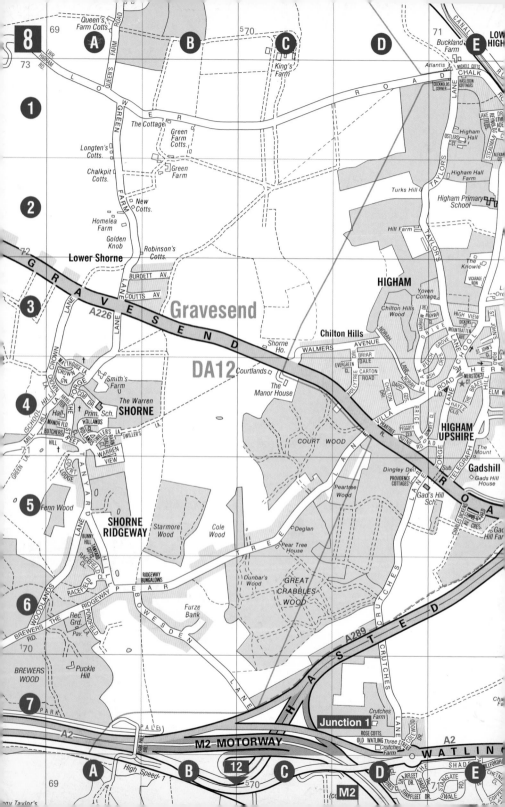

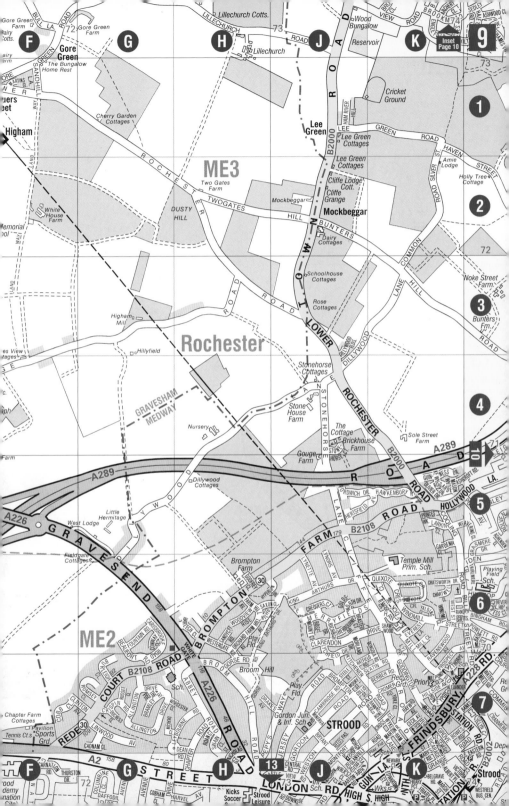

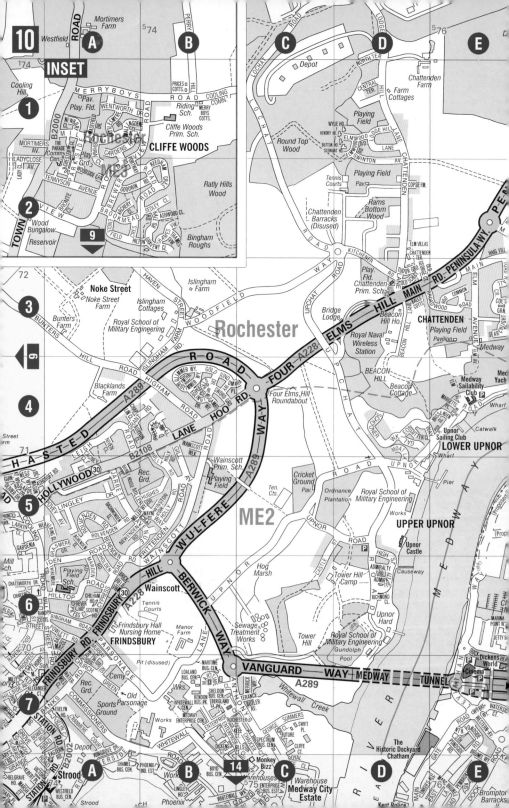

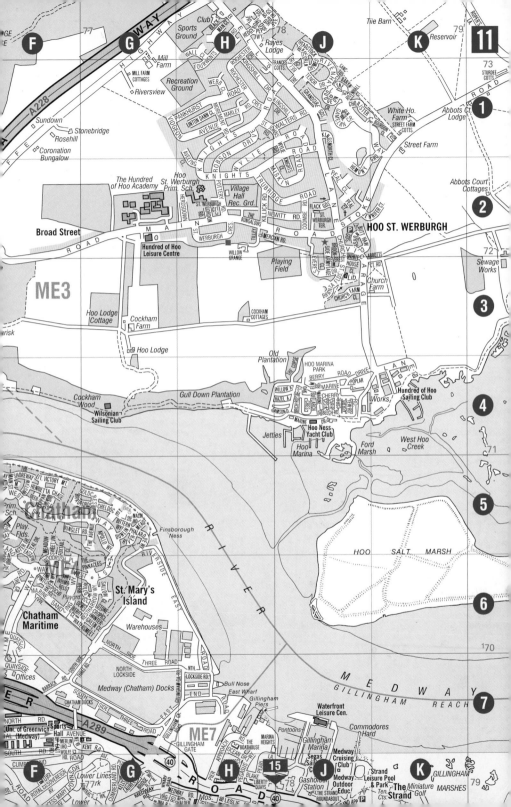

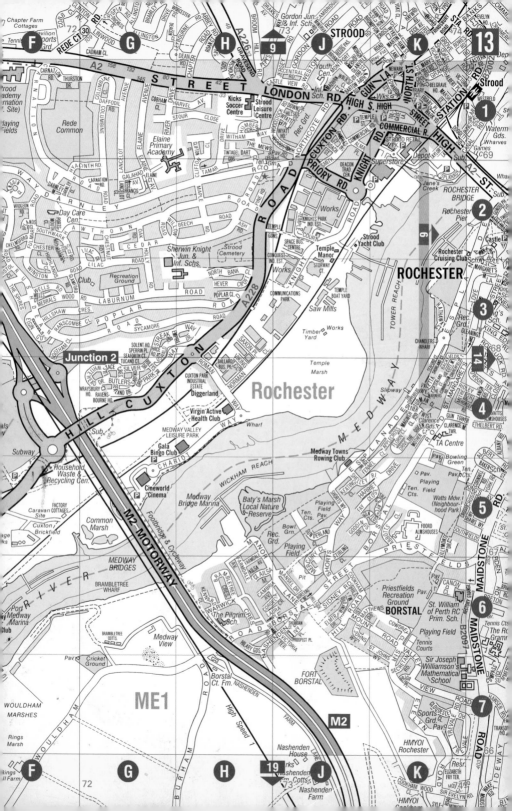

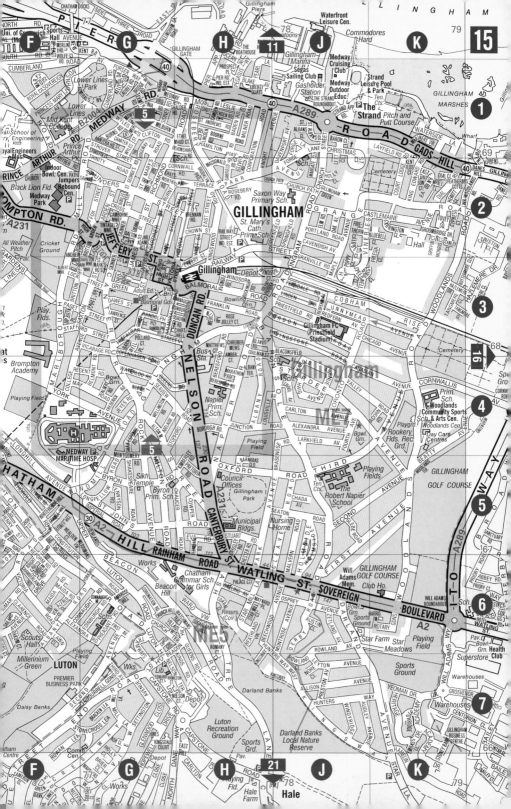

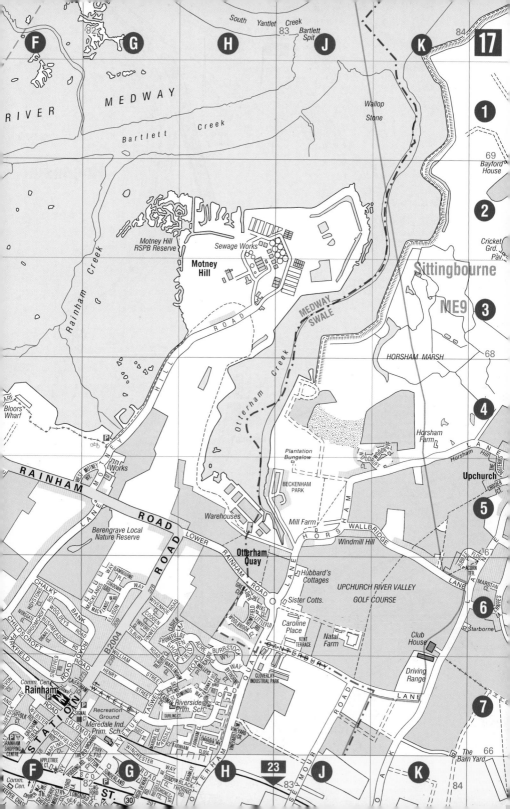

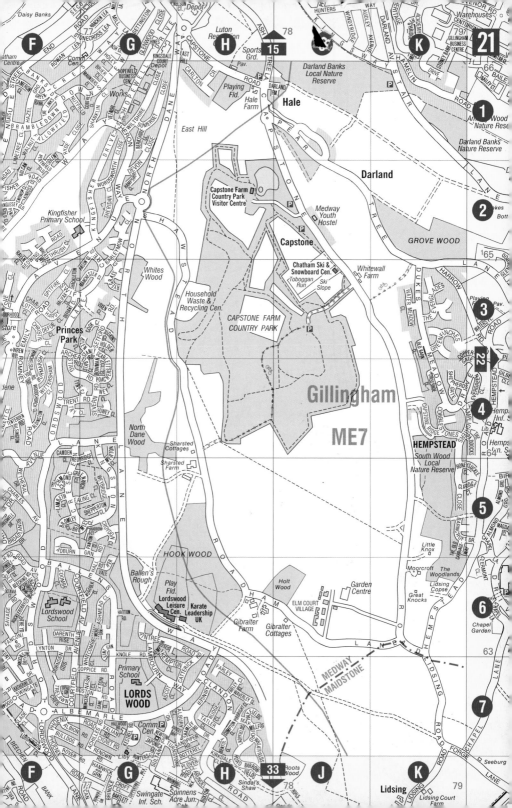

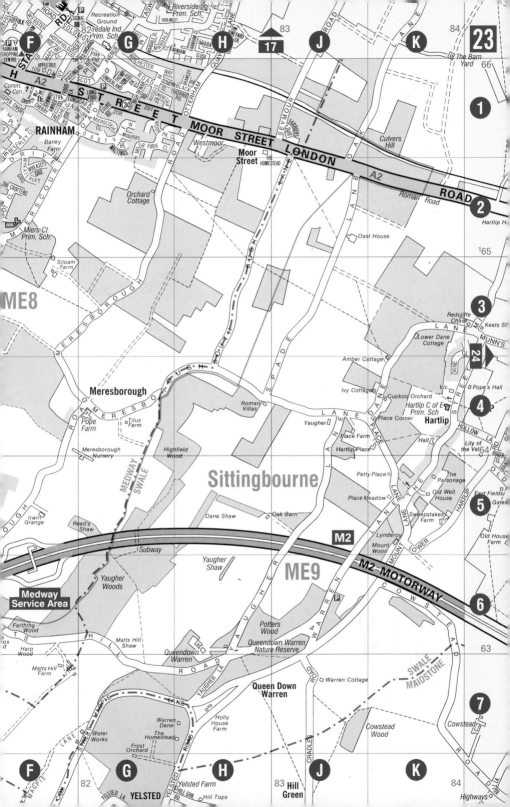

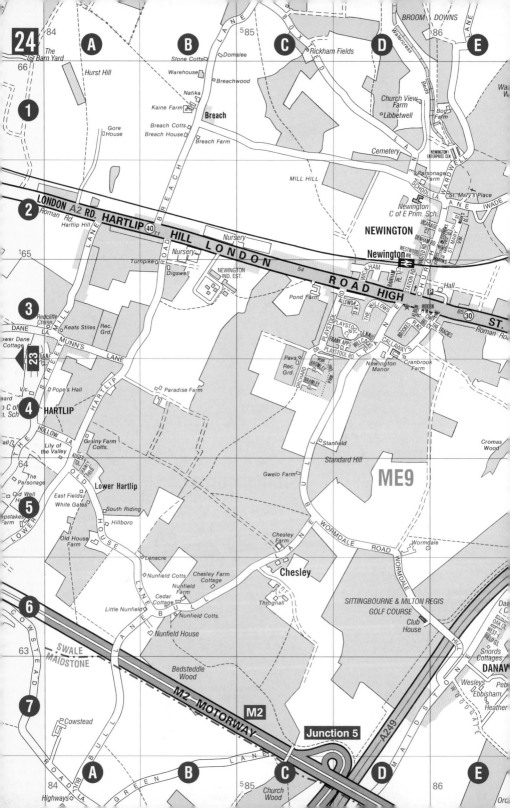

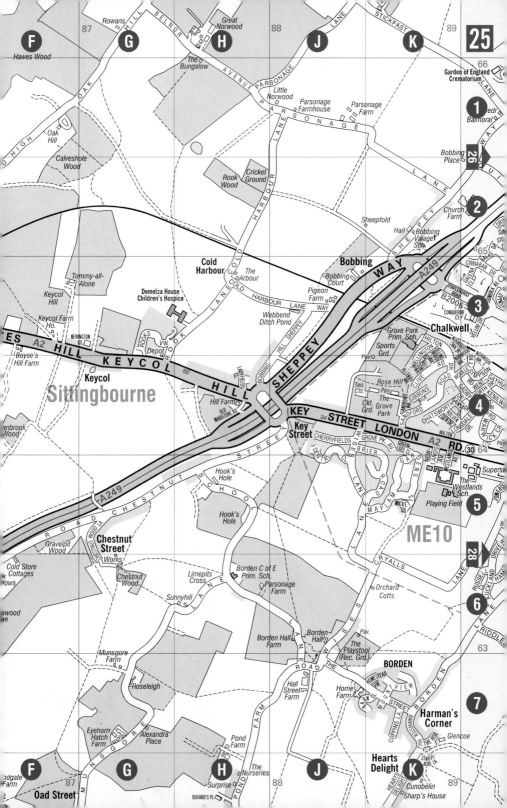

F
G
H
J
K

Warehouse

92

RIDHAM DOCK

Works

Works

Wall

Ridham

Jetty

HES

Works

Works

Tanks

Jetty

Kemsley Marshes

Kemsley Mill

Works

Kemsley Down

sley Down

stle Rough

Kemsley Marshes

Milton Creek

Works

WATERVIEW BUSINESS PARK

CASTLE

ROAD

FAIRWAY BUSINESS PARK

EUROLINK BUSINESS PK

THE GLENMORE CENTRE

Works

ANCHOR BUS. PK

Sittingbourne FC

CASTLE

RD

SWALE

WAY

ISLE OF

SHEPPEY

Sheerness

Kings Hill Farm

Elmley Marshes Nature Reserve

ME12

ELMLEY ISLAND

Sharfleet Creek

Elmley Reach

THE

SWALE

The Lilies

ME9

Little Murston

Tonge Corner Farm

Woods Cottages

Tonge Corner

Tonge Corner Cottages

CHURCH RD

BLACKETTS RD

Chenes Court

F
G
H
J
K

29

93

93

94

68

67

66

165

94

1
2
3
4
5
6
7

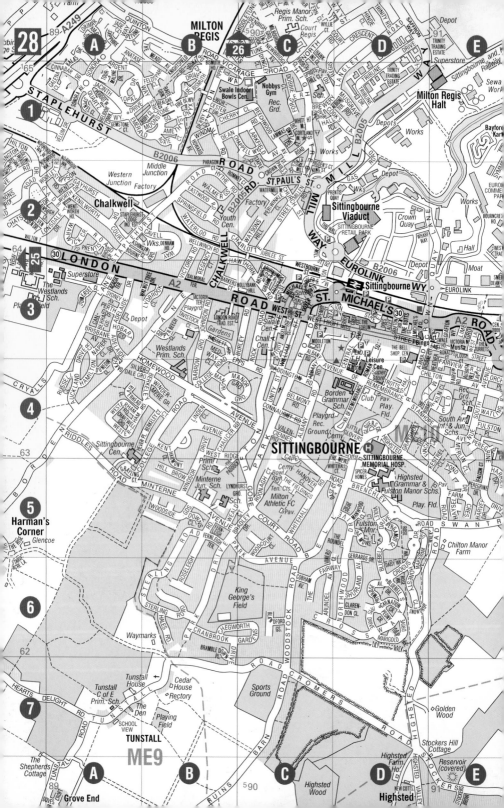

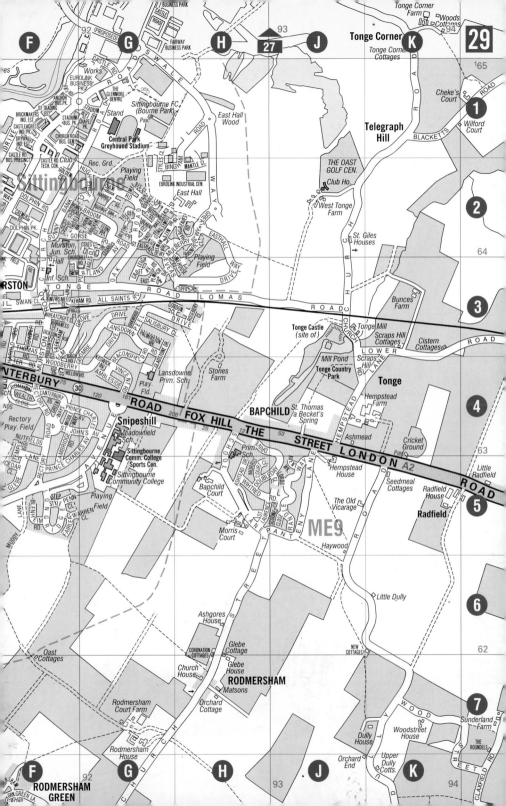

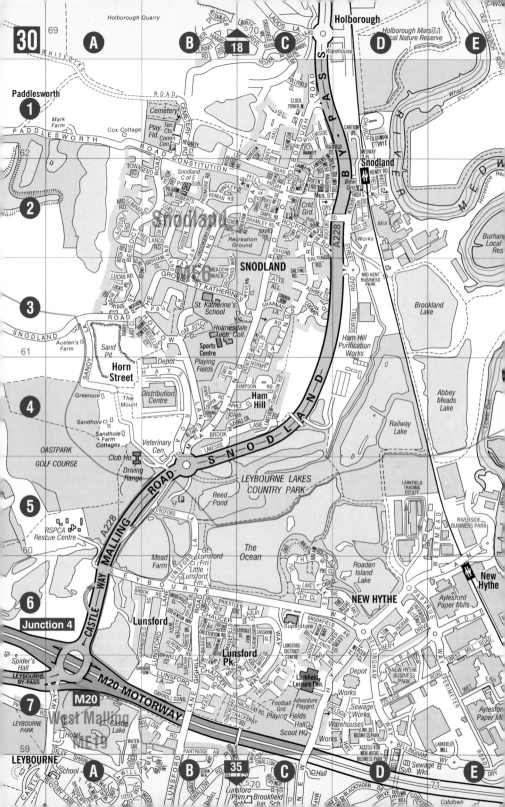

Burham Common

F G H 19 73 J K 31

Lord Lees

74

Burham Court

Rochester

ME1

Aylesford

ME20

Burham Down (Nature Reserve)

Blue Bell Picnic

62

1

2

3

32 61

4

5

160

6

Pratling Street

7

Eccles

Aylesford Sand & Gravel Pit

The Friars (Aylesford Priory)

Millhall

36

AYLESFORD

F G H J K

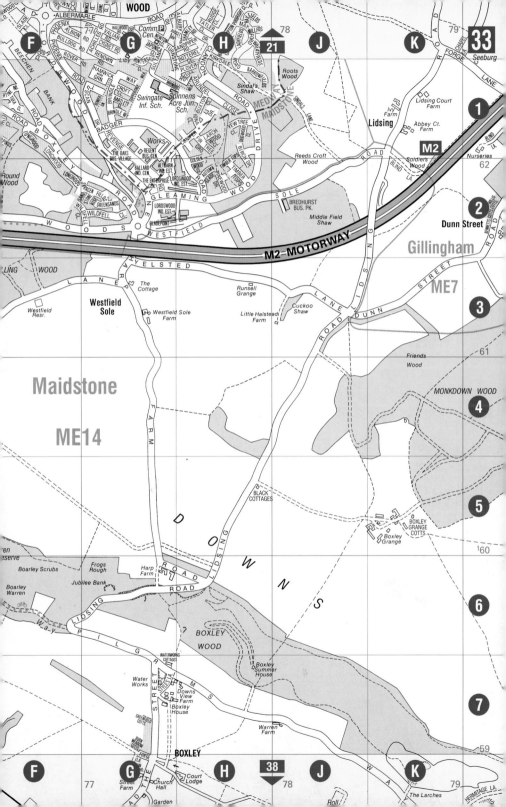

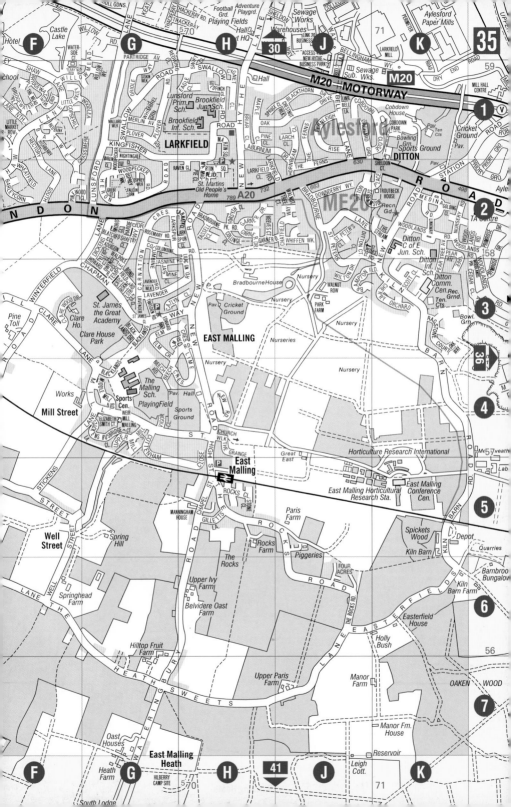

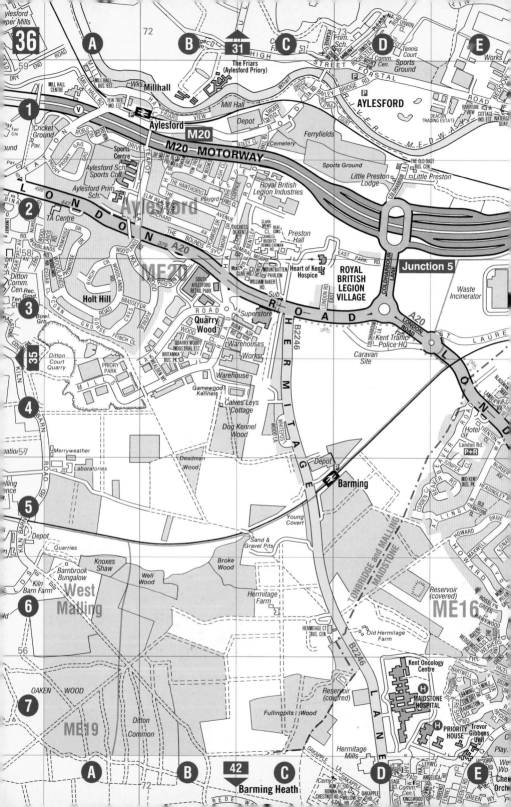

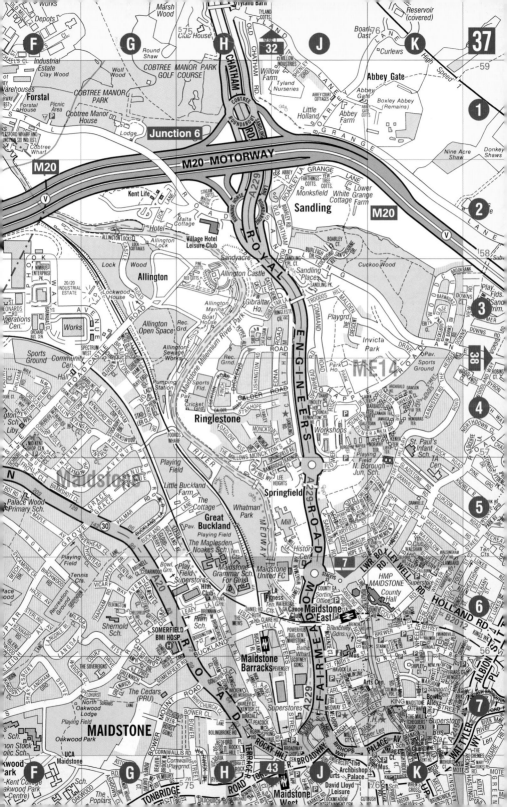

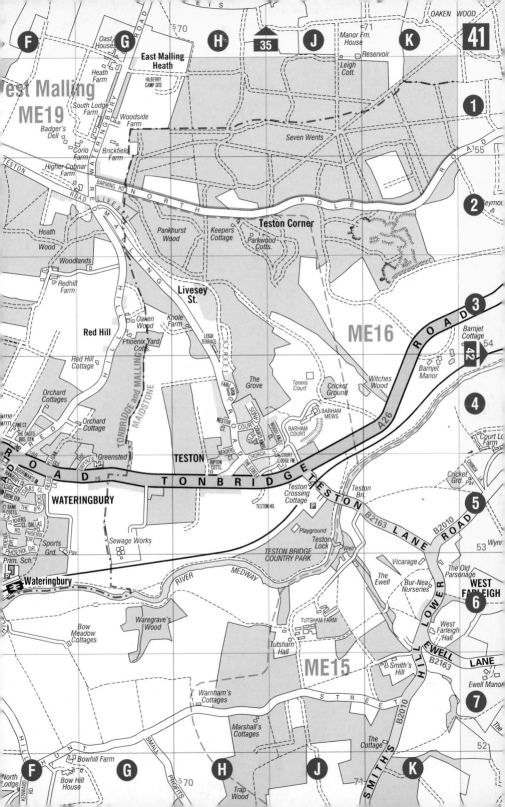

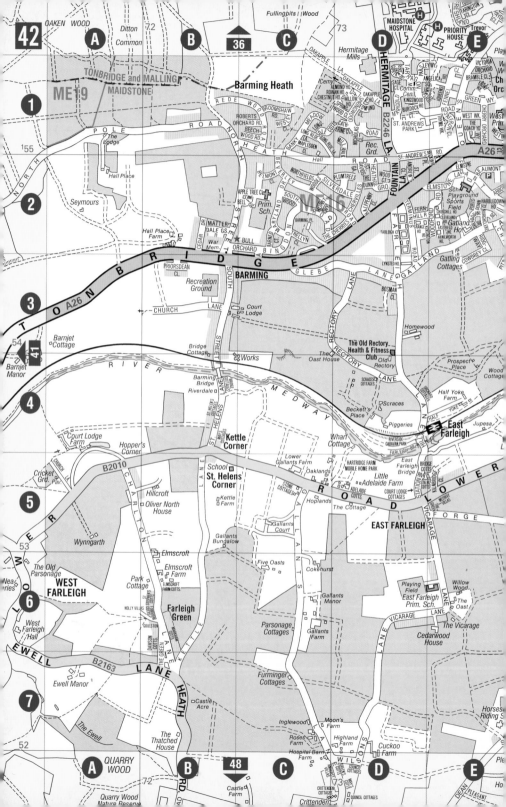

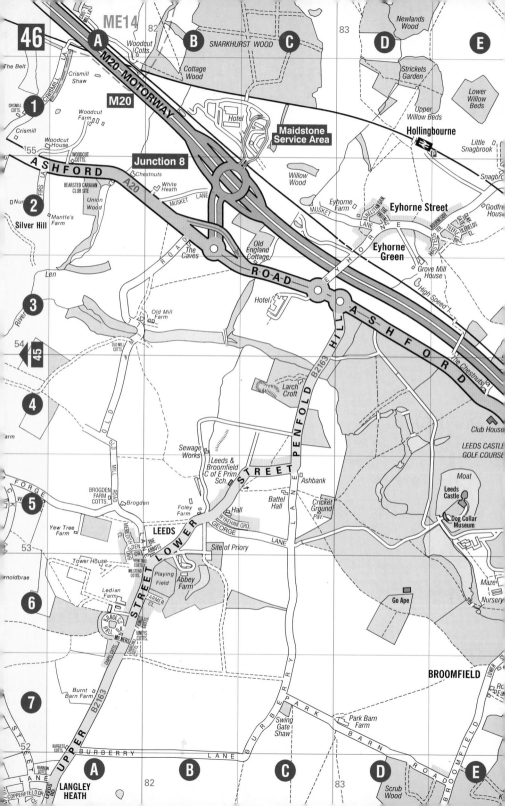

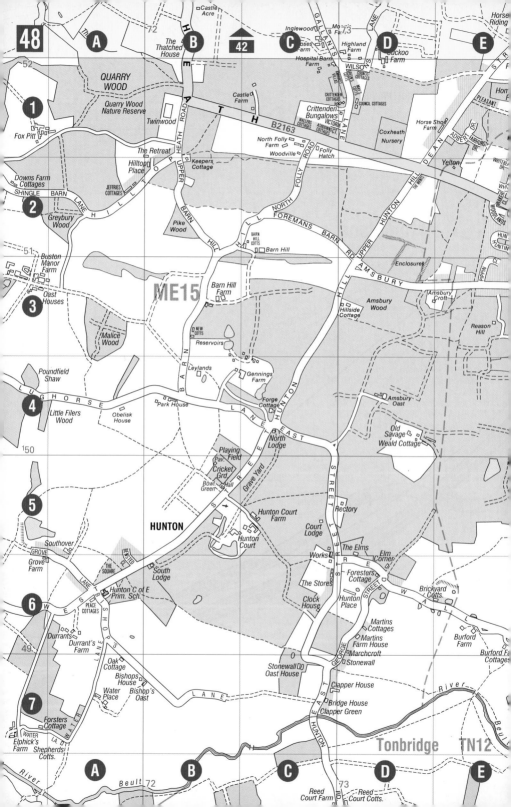

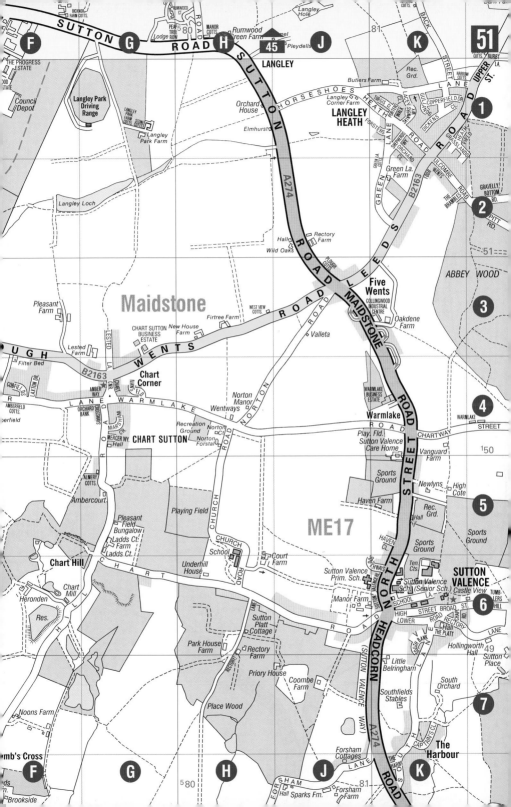

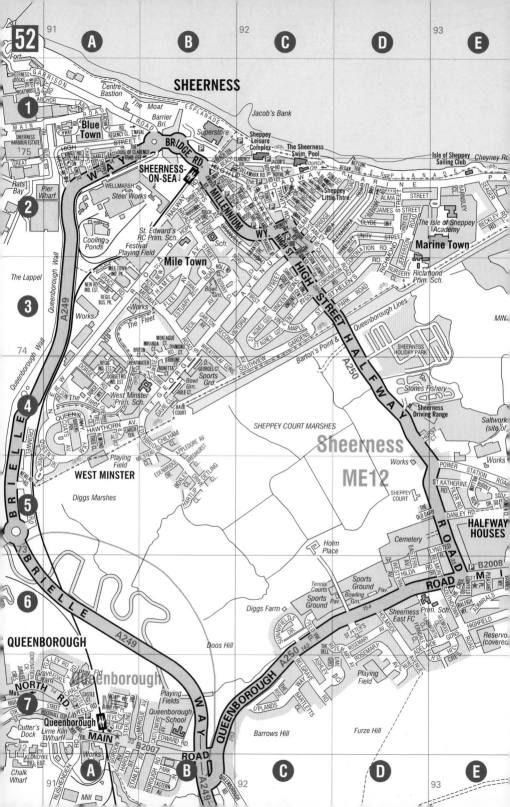

INDEX

Including Streets, Places & Areas, Hospitals etc., Industrial Estates,
Selected Flats & Walkways, Service Areas, Stations and Selected Places of Interest.

HOW TO USE THIS INDEX

1. Each street name is followed by its Postcode District, then by its Locality abbreviation(s) and then by its map reference;
e.g. **Abingdon Rd.** ME16: Barm . . . .2C **42** is in the ME16 Postcode District and the Barming Locality and is to be found in square 2C on page **42**.
The page number is shown in bold type.

2. A strict alphabetical order is followed in which Av., Rd., St., etc. (though abbreviated) are read in full and as part of the street name;
e.g. **Brook La.** appears after **Brooklands Rd.** but before **Brooklyn Paddock**

3. Streets and a selection of flats and walkways that cannot be shown on the mapping, appear in the index with the thoroughfare to which they are connected shown in brackets; e.g. **Aintree Ho.** ME15: Maid . . . .6E **44** (off Epsom Cl.)

4. Addresses that are in more than one part are referred to as not continuous.

5. Places and areas are shown in the index in BLUE TYPE and the map reference is to the actual map square in which the town centre or area is located and not to the place name shown on the map; e.g. **BAPCHILD** 5H **29**

6. An example of a selected place of interest is **Dog Collar Mus.** 5E **46**

7. An example of a station is **Aylesford Station (Rail)** . . . .1B **36**, also included is Park & Ride.
e.g. **London Road (Maidstone) (Park & Ride)** 4E **36**

8. Service Areas are shown in the index in BOLD CAPITAL TYPE; e.g. **MAIDSTONE SERVICE AREA** 1C **46**

9. An example of a Hospital, Hospice or selected Healthcare Facility is **ALEXANDRA SPIRE HOSPITAL** 2E **32**

10. Map references for entries that appear on large scale pages **4-7** are shown first, with small scale map references shown in brackets;
e.g. **Abbeville Ho.** ME1: Roch 7C **6** (4A **14**)

GENERAL ABBREVIATIONS

All. : Alley	**Dr.** : Drive	**Lit.** : Little	**Shop.** : Shopping
App. : Approach	**E.** : East	**Lwr.** : Lower	**Sth.** : South
Arc. : Arcade	**Ent.** : Enterprise	**Mnr.** : Manor	**Sq.** : Square
Av. : Avenue	**Est.** : Estate	**Mkt.** : Market	**Sta.** : Station
Blvd. : Boulevard	**Fld.** : Field	**Mdw.** : Meadow	**St.** : Street
Bri. : Bridge	**Flds.** : Fields	**Mdws.** : Meadows	**Ter.** : Terrace
Bldgs. : Buildings	**Gdn.** : Garden	**M.** : Mews	**Twr.** : Tower
Bungs. : Bungalows	**Gdns.** : Gardens	**Mt.** : Mount	**Trad.** : Trading
Bus. : Business	**Ga.** : Gate	**Mus.** : Museum	**Up.** : Upper
Cen. : Centre	**Gt.** : Great	**Nth.** : North	**Va.** : Vale
Cir. : Circus	**Grn.** : Green	**Pde.** : Parade	**Vw.** : View
Cl. : Close	**Gro.** : Grove	**Pk.** : Park	**Vs.** : Villas
Comn. : Common	**Hgts.** : Heights	**Pas.** : Passage	**Vis.** : Visitors
Cnr. : Corner	**Ho.** : House	**Pav.** : Pavilion	**Wlk.** : Walk
Cott. : Cottage	**Ho's.** : Houses	**Pl.** : Place	**W.** : West
Cotts. : Cottages	**Ind.** : Industrial	**Pct.** : Precinct	**Yd.** : Yard
Ct. : Court	**Info.** : Information	**Ri.** : Rise	
Cres. : Crescent	**Junc.** : Junction	**Rd.** : Road	
Cft. : Croft	**La.** : Lane	**Rdbt.** : Roundabout	

LOCALITY ABBREVIATIONS

Addtn : **Addington**	E Far : **East Farleigh**	Lord W : **Lords Wood**	Sit : **Sittingbourne**
Alltn : **Allington**	E Mal : **East Malling**	Lwr Hal : **Lower Halstow**	Snod : **Snodland**
Aylfd : **Aylesford**	E Peck : **East Peckham**	Lud'n : **Luddesdown**	S'bry : **Stockbury**
Bap : **Bapchild**	Eccl : **Eccles**	Lyn : **Lynsted**	Strood : **Strood**
Barm : **Barming**	Gill : **Gillingham**	Maid : **Maidstone**	Sut V : **Sutton Valence**
Bear : **Bearsted**	Grav'nd : **Gravesend**	Mard : **Marden**	Tstn : **Teston**
Birl : **Birling**	Hall'g : **Halling**	Med E : **Medway City Estate**	Tey : **Teynham**
Blue H : **Blue Bell Hill**	H'shm : **Harrietsham**	Mere : **Mereworth**	T'hm : **Thurnham**
Bob : **Bobbing**	H'lip : **Hartlip**	Minst : **Minster**	Tonge : **Tonge**
B'den : **Borden**	Hpstd : **Hempstead**	Nett : **Nettlestead**	T'stall : **Tunstall**
Bou Mo : **Boughton Monchelsea**	High'm : **Higham**	N'tn : **Newington**	Upc : **Upchurch**
Boxl : **Boxley**	Holl : **Hollingbourne**	Off : **Offham**	Upnor : **Upnor**
B'hst : **Bredhurst**	Hoo W : **Hoo St Werburgh**	Otham : **Otham**	Wain : **Wainscott**
Broom : **Broomfield**	Hunt : **Hunton**	Parkw : **Parkwood**	W'slade : **Walderslade**
Burh : **Burham**	Iwade : **Iwade**	Pen H : **Penenden Heath**	W'bury : **Wateringbury**
Cha S : **Chart Sutton**	Kems'y : **Kemsley**	Queen : **Queenborough**	Weav : **Weavering**
Chat'm : **Chatham**	Kings H : **Kings Hill**	Rain : **Rainham**	W Far : **West Farleigh**
C'den : **Chattenden**	Kgswd : **Kingswood**	Roch : **Rochester**	W Mal : **West Malling**
Cliffe : **Cliffe**	L'ly : **Langley**	Rod : **Rodmersham**	Wigm : **Wigmore**
Cli W : **Cliffe Woods**	Lark : **Larkfield**	Rya : **Ryarsh**	Woul : **Wouldham**
Cox : **Coxheath**	Leeds : **Leeds**	St Mary : **St Mary's Island**	Yald : **Yalding**
Cux : **Cuxton**	Leyb : **Leybourne**	S'lng : **Sandling**	
Det : **Detling**	Lint : **Linton**	S'ness : **Sheerness**	
Dit : **Ditton**	Loose : **Loose**	Shorne : **Shorne**	

A

1st Bowl	**Abberley Pk.**	**Abbey Brewery Ct.**	**Abbey Ga. Cotts.** ME14: S'lng . . .1J **37**
Chatham 4C **4** (4D **14**)	ME14: Maid 5B **38**	ME19: W Mal 3D **34**	**Abbey Rd.** ME2: Strood 7H **9**
20/20 Ind. Est.	**Abbeville Ho.**	**Abbey Cl.** ME12: Minst 6K **53**	ME8: Gill 6A **16**
ME16: Alltn 3F **37**	ME1: Roch 7C **6** (4A **14**)	**Abbey Ct.** ME14: S'lng 2J **37**	**Abbeyview Dr.** ME12: Minst 6H **53**
		Abbey Ct. Cotts. ME14: S'lng 1J **37**	**Abbey Wood Rd.**
		ABBEY GATE 1J **37**	ME19: Kings H 6B **34**
			Abbots, The ME17: Leeds 5B **46**

Abbots Fld.—Aylesford Station (Rail)

Abbots Fld. ME16: Maid 2E **42**
Abbotts Cl. ME1: Roch 5K **13**
Abbotts Ct. Rd.
ME3: Hoo W 2K **11**
Abelyn Av. ME10: Sit 2G **29**
Aberdeen Ho. ME15: Maid 5D **44**
Abery Dr. ME20: Lark 6D **30**
Abigail Cres. ME5: W'slade 1E **32**
Abingdon M. ME19: W Mal 3D **34**
Abingdon Rd. ME16: Barm 2C **42**
Abinger Dr. ME5: Lord W 7H **21**
Absolam Ct. ME8: Gill 6C **16**
Acacia Ter. ME10: Sit 3A **28**
Academy Dr. ME7: Gill 7K **15**
Access 4:20 New Hythe Bus. Pk.
ME20: Lark 7D **30**
Achilles Rd. ME5: Lord W 7G **21**
Acorn Bus. Cen.
ME16: Maid 2F **43**
Acorn Gro. ME20: Dit 3A **36**
Acorn Pl. ME15: Maid 6D **44**
Acorn Rd. ME7: Gill 4K **15**
Acorn St. ME12: S'ness 3C **52**
Acorn Ter. ME9: Upc 6K **17**
Acorn Wharf Rd.
ME1: Roch 3C **6** (2A **14**)
Acre Cl. ME1: Roch 7C **14**
Acre Gro. ME2: Hall'g 5C **18**
Adam Cl. ME17: Cox 2G **49**
Adbert Dr. ME15: E Far 1E **48**
Addington Rd. ME10: Sit 4C **28**
Addison Cl. ME19: E Mal 2G **35**
Adelaide, The ME3: High'm 1E **8**
Adelaide Cotts. ME15: E Far 5D **42**
Adelaide Dr. ME10: Sit 3A **28**
Adelaide Gdns.
ME12: Minst 6D **52**
Adelaide Rd. ME7: Gill . . .7H **5** (4G **15**)
Aden Ter. ME14: Maid 4J **37**
Adisham Dr. ME16: Alltn 4E **36**
Adisham Grn. ME10: Kems'y 6D **26**
Admiral Moore Dr.
ME20: Aylfd 2C **36**
Admirals Wlk. ME4: Chat'm 1D **14**
ME5: Lord W 6F **21**
ME7: Gill 1G **5** (1G **15**)
ME12: Minst 6E **52**
Admiralty Rd. ME2: Upnor 6D **10**
Admiralty Ter. ME2: Upnor 6D **10**
ME7: Gill 1E **14**
Admiral Way ME19: Kings H 3B **40**
Afghan Rd.
ME4: Chat'm 5A **4** (4C **14**)
Agate Ct. ME10: Sit 1B **28**
Ailsa Ct. ME1: Roch 6H **13**
Ailsa M. ME1: Roch 6H **13**
Aimes Ho. ME15: Loose 2J **49**
Aintree Ho. *ME15: Maid 6E 44*
(off Epsom Cl.)
Aintree Rd. ME5: Lord W 6G **21**
Ajax Rd. ME1: Roch 1A **20**
Alamein Av. ME5: Chat'm 2D **20**
Albany Rd. ME1: Roch 4A **14**
ME4: Chat'm 6F **15**
ME7: Gill 7K **5** (4H **15**)
ME10: Sit 3C **28**
Albany St. ME14: Maid . . .1K **7** (6A **38**)
Albany Ter.
ME4: Chat'm 5A **4** (4C **14**)
ME7: Gill 6K **5** (4H **15**)
Albatross Av. ME2: Strood 1E **12**
Albemarle Rd. ME5: Lord W 7F **21**
Albert Mnr. ME7: Gill 4F **5** (3F **15**)
Albert Pl. ME2: Strood . . .1A **6** (1K **13**)
Albert Reed Gdns.
ME15: Maid 2H **43**
Albert Rd. ME1: Roch 4A **14**
ME4: Chat'm 7D **4** (5E **14**)
ME7: Gill 6G **5** (4G **15**)
Albert St. ME14: Maid 5J **37**
Albion Ho. *ME15: Maid 3H 43*
(off Wharfdale Sq.)
Albion Pl. ME2: Upnor 4E **10**
ME9: N'tn 3D **24**
ME12: S'ness 2C 52
(off High St.)
ME14: Maid 4K **7** (7K **37**)
Albion Rd. ME5: Lord W 7F **21**
Albion Ter. ME10: Sit 1D **28**
Albury Cl. ME5: Lord W 7H **21**
Alchins Cotts. ME17: Lint 3H **49**
Alder Cl. ME12: S'ness 4A **52**
Aldershot Rd. ME5: Chat'm 2E **20**
Alderwick Gro.
ME19: Kings H 1D **40**
Aldington Cl. ME5: W'slade 4F **21**
Aldington La. ME14: T'hm 3J **39**
Aldington Rd. ME14: Bear 7E **38**
Aldon Cl. ME14: Maid 5B **38**
Aldon Ct. ME14: Maid 5B **38**
Alefe Way ME9: Iwade 3B **26**
Alexander Cotts. ME3: High'm 1E **8**
Alexander Ct. ME2: Strood 7K **9**
Alexander Gro.
ME19: Kings H 1B **40**
(not continuous)
Alexandra Av. ME7: Gill . . .7K **5** (4J **15**)
Alexandra Cl. ME10: Sit 7C **26**
Alexandra Glen
ME5: W'slade 1E **32**
Alexandra Rd. ME4: Chat'm 6F **15**
ME12: S'ness 2D **52**
ALEXANDRA SPIRE HOSPITAL
. . . . .2E **32**
Alexandra St.
ME14: Maid 1H **7** (5J **37**)
Alex Hughes Cl. ME6: Snod 4B **30**
Alfred Cl. ME4: Chat'm 6F **15**
Alfriston Gro. ME19: Kings H . . .1D **40**
Alisander Cl. ME6: Snod 7B **18**
Alkham Rd. ME14: Maid 7B **38**
All Angels Cl. ME16: Maid 1G **43**
Allenby Wlk. ME10: Sit 4K **25**
Allen Cl. ME5: Lord W 3G **21**
Allen Ct. ME12: Minst 7G **53**
Allen St. ME14: Maid 1K **7** (6A **38**)
ALLINGTON **3G 37**
Allington Dr. ME2: Strood 7G **9**
Allington Gdns.
ME18: W'bury 5E **40**
Allington Locks ME16: Alltn 2G **37**
Allington Rd. ME8: Gill 5A **16**
Allington Way ME16: Alltn 5E **36**
Allison Av. ME7: Gill 7J **15**
Allnutt Mill Cl. ME15: Maid 2H **43**
All Saints Church
Maidstone **5H 7**
All Saints Cl. ME9: Iwade 2C **26**
All Saints Rd. ME10: Sit 3G **29**
Allsworth Cl. ME9: N'tn 3D **24**
Alma Pl. ME2: Strood 1J **13**
Alma Rd. ME12: S'ness 2C **52**
ME19: W Mal 3B **34**
ME20: Eccl 4H **31**
Alma St. ME12: S'ness 2D **52**
Alma St. Pas. *ME12: S'ness 2D 52*
(off Richmond St.)
Almery Cotts. ME17: Cha S 5G **51**
Almond Gro. ME7: Hpstd 5A **22**
Almond Ho. ME16: Barm 1D **42**
Almonds, The ME14: Bear 7F **39**
Almond Tree Cl.
ME12: S'ness 4A **52**
Almon Pl. ME1: Roch 6D **6** (3B **14**)
Alpha Cl. ME19: Kings H 1E **40**
Alston Cl. ME12: Minst 5J **53**
Altbarn Ind. Est.
ME5: Lord W 2G **33**
Alton Av. ME19: Kings H 1B **40**
Alton M. ME7: Gill 7H **5** (4G **15**)
Amanda Cl. ME5: W'slade 6D **20**
Amber Ct. ME7: Gill 5K **5** (3H **15**)
Amberfield Cotts.
ME17: Cha S 4F **51**
Amber Grn. Cotts.
ME17: Bou Mo 4D **50**
Amber La. ME17: Cha S 4E **50**
ME19: Kings H 1E **40**
Amber Ri. ME10: Sit 7A **26**
Amber Way ME17: Cha S 4G **51**
Ambleside ME10: Sit 4G **29**
Ambley Grn. ME8: Gill 1A **22**
Ambley Rd. ME8: Gill 7A **16**
Ambley Wood Local Nature Reserve
. . . .**1A 22**
Ambrose Hill ME5: Chat'm 6G **15**
Ames Av. ME14: Bear 7F **39**
Ames Way *ME19: Kings H 1C 40*
(off Orient Ct.)
Amethyst Av. ME5: Chat'm 3C **20**
Amethyst Dr. ME10: Sit 1B **28**
Amethyst Ho. *ME10: Sit 1B 28*
(off Amethyst Dr.)
AMF Bowling
Maidstone **3K 7** (**7K 37**)
Amherst Cl. ME16: Maid 7G **37**
Amherst Hill ME7: Gill . . .1D **4** (2E **14**)
Amherst Redoubt
ME7: Gill 2D **4** (3E **14**)
Amherst Rd. ME1: Roch 5B **14**
Amhurst Vs. ME15: E Far 1C **48**
Amisse Dr. ME6: Snod 7C **18**
Amsbury Rd. ME15: Hunt 3D **48**
ME17: Cox 3D **48**
Anatase Cl. ME10: Sit 7A **26**
Anchorage Ho.
ME4: Chat'm 4A **4** (3C **14**)
Anchor Bus. Pk. ME10: Sit 1F **29**
Anchor Ho. ME1: Roch 7A **6**
Anchor La. ME12: S'ness 1A **52**
Anchor Rd. ME1: Roch 7A **14**
Andover Wlk. ME15: Maid 6E **44**
Andrew Broughton Way
ME14: Maid 4K **7** (7A **38**)
Andrew Mnr. ME7: Gill 3F **5** (2F **15**)
Andrews Wlk. ME10: Sit 4K **25**
Anerley Cl. ME16: Alltn 4G **37**
Angelica Sq. ME16: Maid 1E **42**
Anglesey Av. ME15: Maid 6K **43**
Anglesey Cl. ME5: Chat'm 2F **21**
Anisa Cl. ME19: Kings H 1C **40**
Anne Figg Ct.
ME1: Roch 7C **6** (4A **14**)
Annie Rd. ME6: Snod 4B **30**
Annvera Ho. ME7: Gill . . .1G **5** (1G **15**)
Ansell Av. ME4: Chat'm 6E **14**
Anselm Cl. ME10: Sit 3C **28**
Anson Av. ME19: Kings H 1A **40**
Anson Cl. ME5: Lord W 3G **21**
Anthony's Way ME2: Med E 7B **10**
Apni Haweli ME4: Chat'm 5C **4**
Apollo Way ME4: St Mary 5G **11**
Appleby Cl. ME1: Roch 2B **20**
Apple Cl. ME6: Snod 4B **30**
Applecross Cl. ME1: Roch 4K **13**
Appledore Av.
ME12: S'ness 4B **52**
Appledore Ct. ME16: Alltn 4F **37**
Appledore Rd. ME8: Gill 5A **16**
Appleford Dr. ME12: Minst 5F **53**
Apple Tree Cl. ME16: Barm 2C **42**
Appletree Ct. ME8: Rain 1F **23**
Archbishops Cres. ME7: Gill 2A **16**
Archbishop's Palace, The
Maidstone **5H 7** (**1J 43**)
Archer Ct. ME10: Kems'y 4D **26**
Archer Rd. ME5: Lord W 3F **21**
Archery Cl. ME3: Cli W 2A **10**
Archibald Ho. ME14: Maid 4K **37**
Archway Ct. ME2: Strood 1A **6**
Archway Rd. ME12: S'ness 1A **52**
(not continuous)
Arden Bus. Pk.
ME2: Med E 1E **6** (1B **14**)
Ardenlee Dr. ME14: Maid 6A **38**
Arden St. ME7: Gill 3G **5** (2G **15**)
Arethusa Rd. ME1: Roch 1A **20**
Argent Ter. ME5: W'slade 4D **20**
Argent Way ME10: Sit 1A **28**
Argyle Cl. ME1: Roch 1C **20**
Arlott Cl. ME14: Maid 5J **37**
Armada Ct. ME4: Chat'm 7C **14**
Armada Way
ME4: Chat'm 6B **4** (5D **14**)
Armstrong Rd.
ME15: Maid 3K **43**
Armytage Cl. ME3: Hoo W 3J **11**
Arnhem Dr. ME5: Chat'm 2D **20**
Arnolde Cl. ME2: Med E 1C **14**
Arran Grn. ME2: Strood 2E **12**
Arran Rd. ME15: Maid 6K **43**
Art at the Centre
Sittingbourne **3E 28**
Arthur Rd. ME1: Roch 5B **14**
ME8: Gill 1D **22**
Arthur St. ME10: Sit 3C **28**
Arundel Av. ME10: Sit 6C **28**
Arundel Cl. ME5: Lord W 1H **33**
Arundel Sq.
ME15: Maid 7G **7** (2J **43**)
Arundel St.
ME14: Maid 5J **37**
Ascot Cl. ME5: Lord W 7G **21**
Ascot Ho. *ME15: Maid 6E 44*
(off Epsom Cl.)
Ashbee Cl. ME6: Snod 3C **30**
Ashburnham Rd.
ME14: Pen H 3A **38**
Ashby Cl. ME2: Hall'g 5C **18**
Ash Cl. ME5: Chat'm 7G **15**
ME8: Gill 5B **16**
ME20: Aylfd 2B **36**
Ash Cres. ME3: High'm 4E **8**
Ashcroft Rd. ME3: Wain 5K **9**
Ashdown Cl. ME16: Maid 1G **43**
Ashdowns Cotts.
ME15: E Far 1C **48**
Ashenden Cl. ME2: Wain 5A **10**
Ashford Rd.
ME14: Bear, Maid, Weav . . .7A **38**
ME15: Bear 1G **45**
ME17: H'shm, Holl 1H **45**
Ash Gro. ME16: Alltn 5F **37**
Ashington Cl. ME10: Sit 2A **28**
Ash La. ME12: Minst 3G **53**
Ashleigh Gdns. ME5: Blue H 7B **20**
Ashley Cl. ME12: Minst 7C **52**
Ashley Rd. ME8: Gill 6C **16**
Ashmead Cl. ME5: Lord W 6G **21**
Ash Rd. ME2: Strood 2H **13**
Ashtead Dr. ME9: Bap 5H **29**
Ashton Way ME19: W Mal 2E **34**
Ash Tree Gdns. ME14: Weav 5E **38**
Ashtree Ho. *ME10: Sit 4F 29*
(off Woodberry Dr.)
Ash Tree La. ME5: Chat'm 6H **15**
Ashurst Pl. ME8: Gill 1E **22**
Ashurst Rd. ME14: Maid 6B **38**
Ashwood Cl. ME3: Cli W 2B **10**
Aspen Dr. ME12: Minst 7H **53**
Aspen Way ME5: W'slade 5C **20**
Aspian Dr. ME17: Cox 2G **49**
Asquith Rd. ME8: Wigm 3C **22**
Association Wlk.
ME1: Roch 2A **20**
Aster Dr. ME4: St Mary 5F **11**
Aster Rd. ME3: Hoo W 4J **11**
ME12: Minst 7H **53**
Astley St. ME14: Maid . . .3K **7** (7K **37**)
Astley Ter. ME15: Maid . . .5K **7** (1A **44**)
Aston Cl. ME5: W'slade 7E **20**
Astor Pk. ME16: Maid 1G **43**
Athelstan Grn. ME17: Holl 2D **46**
Athelstan Rd. ME4: Chat'm 6D **14**
Atkins Hill ME17: Bou Mo 1A **50**
Atlanta Ct. ME4: Chat'm 5B **14**
Atlas Cl. ME19: Kings H 1E **40**
Attlee Cotts. ME2: Hall'g 3C **18**
Attlee Way ME10: Sit 6C **26**
Aubretia Wlk. ME10: Sit 4E **28**
Auckland Dr. ME10: Sit 4A **28**
Auden Rd. ME20: Lark 7C **30**
Audley Av. ME7: Gill 7J **15**
Audley Cl. ME16: Alltn 6E **36**
Auger Cl. ME9: H'lip 4A **24**
Augusta Cl. ME7: Gill 1G **15**
Augustine Rd. ME12: Minst 4H **53**
Auriga ME1: Roch 7D **6**
Austell Mnr. ME7: Gill 3G **5**
Austen Way ME20: Lark 6B **30**
Austin Cl. ME5: Chat'm 6J **15**
ME10: Kems'y 6E **26**
Austin Hgts. ME16: Maid 2F **43**
Autumn Glade ME5: Lord W 2H **33**
Aveling Cl. ME3: Hoo W 1H **11**
Aveling Ct. *ME2: Strood 1K 13*
(off North St.)
Avent Wlk. ME9: Bap 5J **29**
Avenue, The ME4: St Mary 5G **11**
ME20: Aylfd 2B **36**
Avenue of Remembrance
ME10: Sit 4C **28**
Avenue Theatre
Sittingbourne **4D 28**
Averenches Rd. ME14: Weav 6E **38**
Averenches Rd. Sth.
ME14: Weav 7E **38**
Avery Cl. ME15: Maid 3J **43**
Avery La. ME15: Otham 6J **45**
ME17: Leeds 6J **45**
Aviemore Gdns. ME14: Bear 7E **38**
Avington Cl. ME15: Maid 3J **43**
Avocet Wlk. ME5: Lord W 7G **21**
ME9: Iwade 3C **26**
Avondale Ct. ME14: Weav 6D **38**
Avondale Rd. ME7: Gill . . .4J **5** (3H **15**)
AYLESFORD **1D 36**
Aylesford Cres. ME8: Gill 4B **16**
Aylesford Priory **1B 36**
Aylesford School Sports College
Sports Cen. **1A 36**
Aylesford Station (Rail) **1B 36**

Black Cotts. ME14: Boxl 5H 33
Blacketts Rd. ME9: Tonge ...1K 29
Blacklands ME19: E Mal 4G 35
(not continuous)
Blacklands Dr. ME19: E Mal ...3G 35
Blackman Cl. ME3: Hoo W ...1H 11
Blackmanstone Way
ME16: Alltn 4E 36
Black Rock Gdns. ME7: Hpstd ..5B 22
Blacksmith Dr. ME14: Weav 6C 38
Blackthorn Av. ME5: W'slade ..6E 20
Blackthorn Dr. ME20: Lark 1J 35
Blackthorne Rd. ME8: Rain ...1H 23
Blake Av. ME7: Gill 1H 15
Blake Dr. ME20: Lark 6B 30
Blakeney Cl. ME14: Bear 7G 39
Blaker Av. ME1: Roch 7C 14
Blandford Gdns. ME10: Sit ...6C 28
Blatcher Cl. ME12: Minst 6H 53
Blatchford Cl. ME19: E Mal ...2G 35
Bleakwood Rd.
ME5: W'slade 4D 20
Blean Rd. ME8: Gill 6C 16
Blean Sq. ME14: Maid 5B 38
Blendon Rd. ME14: Maid 6B 38
Blenheim Av. ME14: Chat'm ...6B 14
Blenheim Ct. ME15: Bear 1E 44
Blenheim Rd. ME10: Sit 5F 29
ME19: Kings H 1A 40
Bligh Way ME2: Strood 1E 12
Blind La. ME7: B'hst 1K 33
ME14: Boxl 2K 33
Blockmakers Cl. ME4: Chat'm ..7E 14
Bloomsbury Wlk. ME14: Maid ...3K 7
Bloors La. ME8: Rain 7D 16
(not continuous)
Bloors Wharf Rd. ME8: Rain ...4E 16
Blowers Wood Gro.
ME7: Hpstd 6B 22
Bluebell Cl. ME7: Gill 2K 15
ME12: Minst 7H 53
Bluebell Dr. ME10: Rod, Sit ...6D 28
Blue Bell Hill By-Pass
ME5: Blue H 1A 32
Blue Boar La.
ME1: Roch 5C 6 (3A 14)
Bluecoats Yd. ME15: Maid ...5J 7
BLUE TOWN 1A 52
Bluett St. ME14: Maid ...1K 7 (5K 37)
Blythe Cl. ME10: Sit 2G 29
Blythe Rd. ME15: Maid 7A 38
BOARLEY 7E 32
Boarley Ct. ME14: Maid 2J 37
Boarley La. ME14: S'lng 2J 37
(not continuous)
Boarley Rd. ME14: S'lng 2J 37
Boathouse, The ME7: Gill 7H 11
Boathouse Rd. ME12: S'ness ..1A 52
Boatyard, The ME15: Maid ...2H 43
BOBBING 3J 25
Bobbing Hill ME9: Bob 4H 25
Bob Dunn Health Club 3K 43
Bockingford Ct. ME15: Maid ...4J 43
Bockingford Ho. ME15: Maid ..4J 43
Bockingford La. ME15: Maid ...4J 43
Bockingford Mill Cotts.
ME15: Maid 4J 43
Bodiam Cl. ME8: Gill 5C 16
Bodiam Ct.
ME16: Maid 6G 7 (1J 43)
Bodkins Cl. ME17: Bou Mo ...7C 44
Bodsham Cres. ME15: Bear ..1G 45
Bogarde Dr. ME3: Wain 7K 9
Boley Hill ME1: Roch ...5B 6 (2A 14)
Boleyn Ct. ME7: Gill 2E 14
Bolingbroke Ho.
ME16: Maid 4F 7 (7H 37)
Bolner Cl. ME5: W'slade 7D 20
Bondfield Rd. ME19: E Mal ...3G 35
Bond Rd. ME8: Parkw 5E 22
Bonetta Ct. ME12: S'ness ...4B 52
Bonflower La. ME17: Lint 6F 49
Bonham Dr. ME10: Sit 2E 28
Bonnington Grn. ME8: Gill ...5C 16
Bonnington Rd. ME14: Maid ...5B 38
Boormans Cotts.
ME18: W'bury 5D 40
Boorman's M. ME18: W'bury ...5F 41
Bootham Ct. ME2: Strood 3F 13
Booth Cl. ME6: Snod 7C 18
Booth Rd.
ME4: Chat'm 7C 4 (6D 14)

BORDEN 7K 25
Borden La. ME9: B'den, Sit ...7K 25
ME10: Sit 7K 25
Borough Rd. ME7: Gill ...7J 5 (4H 15)
BORSTAL 6J 13
Borstal M. ME1: Roch 6J 13
Borstal Rd. ME1: Roch 5K 13
Borstal St. ME1: Roch 6J 13
Bosman Cl. ME16: Maid 3D 42
Boston Gdns. ME8: Gill 7C 16
Boston Rd. ME5: Lord W 7G 21
Botany Cl. ME12: S'ness 3B 52
Bottlescrew Hill
ME17: Bou Mo 1A 50
BOUGHTON BOTTOM 7B 50
Boughton Cl. ME8: Gill 5C 16
BOUGHTON GREEN 2A 50
Boughton La. ME15: Maid 5A 44
ME17: Bou Mo, Maid 7A 44
BOUGHTON MONCHELSEA ..2A 50
Boughton Pde. ME15: Maid ...5K 43
Boundary Cl. ME12: Minst ...6K 53
Boundary Rd.
ME4: Chat'm 6A 4 (5B 14)
Bounds, The ME20: Aylfd 2B 36
Bourdon Cl. ME3: Hoo W 1K 11
Bourncrete Ho. ME10: Sit 2E 28
Bourne Ct. ME1: Roch ...6E 6 (3B 14)
Bourne Gro. ME10: Sit 2A 28
Bourneside Ter. ME17: Holl ...2E 46
Bournewood Cl. ME15: Bear ...3E 44
Bournville Av. ME4: Chat'm ...7D 14
Bovarde Av. ME19: Kings H ...1D 40
Bow Bri. ME18: W'bury 6F 41
Bower Cl. ME16: Maid 7H 37
Bower Grn. ME5: Lord W 1G 33
Bower La. ME16: Maid 1H 43
Bower Mt. Rd. ME16: Maid ...7G 37
Bower Pl.
ME16: Maid 5F 7 (1H 43)
Bower St. ME16: Maid 7H 37
Bower Ter. ME16: Maid ...5F 7 (1H 43)
Bowesden La.
DA12: Shorne, Strood 6A 8
Bowes Rd. ME2: Strood ...1A 6 (7K 9)
Bow Hill ME18: W'bury 6E 40
Bowman Cl. ME5: Lord W 4G 21
Bow Rd. ME18: W'bury 6F 41
Bow Ter. ME18: W'bury 5F 41
BOXLEY 1B 38
Boxley Cl. ME12: S'ness 5B 52
ME14: Pen H 3A 38
Boxley Grange Cotts.
ME14: Boxl 5K 33
Boxley Rd. ME5: W'slade 7E 20
ME14: Boxl, Maid, Pen H
................1J 7 (5K 37)
Boxley Warren Local Nature Reserve
......................5E 32
Boxmend Ind. Est.
ME15: Maid 2E 50
Boxted La. ME9: N'tn, Upc 1C 24
Boyces Hill ME9: N'tn 3E 24
Boyd Bus. Cen.
ME2: Med E 1E 6 (1B 14)
Brabourne Av. ME8: Gill 4C 16
Bracken Cl. ME10: Sit 2G 29
Bracken Hill ME5: W'slade ...1E 32
Bracken Lea ME5: Chat'm ...7G 15
Brackley Cl. ME14: Maid 6B 38
Brackwood Cl. ME8: Parkw ...4D 22
Bradbourne La. ME20: Dit 2J 35
Bradbourne Pk. Rd.
ME19: E Mal 2H 35
Braddick Cl. ME16: Maid 7A 44
Bradfields Av. ME5: Chat'm ...3D 20
Bradfields Av. W.
ME5: Chat'm 3D 20
Bradfords Cl. ME4: St Mary ...5F 11
Bradley Dr. ME10: Sit 5C 28
Bradley Rd. ME2: Hall'g 4A 18
Braeburn Way
ME19: Kings H 1C 40
Braes, The ME3: High'm 4E 8
Brake Av. ME5: Chat'm 4C 20
Bramble Cl. ME16: Maid 1E 42
Brambledown ME5: Chat'm ...1F 21
Bramble Down Pl. ME10: Sit ...6B 28
Bramblefield La. ME9: Bob ...5B 26
ME10: Kems'y 5C 26
Brambles, The ME17: L'ly ...2K 51
Brambles Cl. ME12: Minst ...7G 53

Brambletree Cotts.
ME1: Roch 6G 13
Brambletree Cres.
ME1: Roch 6H 13
Brambletree Wharf
ME1: Roch 6G 13
Bramley Cl. ME8: Rain 1H 23
ME9: N'tn 4C 24
Bramley Cres. ME15: Bear ...1E 44
Bramley Gdns. ME17: Cox ...2G 49
Bramley Ri. ME2: Strood 7G 9
Bramley Rd. ME6: Snod 2C 30
Bramley Way ME19: Kings H ...2B 40
Brampton Fld. ME20: Dit 3J 35
Brampton Rd. ME12: Minst ...6J 53
Bransgore Cl. ME8: Gill 2D 22
Branta Flds. ME3: Hoo W 3J 11
Brasenose Rd.
ME7: Gill 7K 5 (5J 15)
Brasier Cl. ME12: Minst 7G 53
Brassey Dr. ME20: Aylfd 3A 36
Brasted Cl. ME2: Strood 6J 9
Braunstone Dr. ME16: Alltn ...3G 37
Bray Gdns. ME15: Maid 7J 43
BREACH 1B 24
Breach La.
ME9: Lwr Hal, Upc 2B 24
Bream Cl. ME20: Lark 5C 30
Brecon Chase ME12: Minst ...5J 53
Bredgar Cl. ME14: Maid 6A 38
Bredgar Rd. ME8: Gill 4A 16
BREDHURST 7B 22
Bredhurst Bus. Pk.
ME14: Boxl 2J 33
Bredhurst Rd. ME8: Wigm ...3B 22
Brenchley Cl. ME1: Roch 6B 14
Brenchley Ho.
ME14: Maid 2H 7 (6J 37)
Brenchley Rd. ME8: Gill 6B 16
ME10: Sit 5B 28
ME15: Maid 7H 7 (2J 43)
Brendon Av. ME5: W'slade ...6E 20
Brennan Ho. ME7: Gill ...3J 5 (2H 15)
Brennan M. ME16: Maid 6H 37
Brent Cl. ME5: Chat'm 4C 20
Brenzett Cl. ME5: W'slade ...4F 21
Brent Rd. ME1: Roch 6A 14
Brett Wlk. ME8: Parkw 5D 22
Brewer Rd. ME3: Cli W 2A 10
Brewers St. ME14: Maid ...2J 7 (6K 37)
Brewery Rd. ME10: Sit 1C 28
Briar Cl. ME20: Lark 1H 35
Briar Dale ME3: High'm 3D 8
Briar Flds. ME14: Weav 5D 38
Briar Ho. ME14: Maid 1K 7
Brice Rd. ME3: High'm 4D 8
Brickfields ME19: Rya 2C 34
Brickmakers Ind. Est.
ME10: Sit 1F 29
Bridge Cotts. ME15: E Far ...5D 42
(River Cl.)
ME15: E Far 4B 42
(St Helens La.)
Bridge Ho. ME1: Roch 7A 6
Bridge Ind. Cen. ME1: Maid ..2H 43
Bridge Mill Way ME15: Maid ...2G 43
Bridge Pl. ME20: Aylfd 1C 36
Bridge Rd. ME1: Roch 6A 14
ME7: Gill 1H 5 (1G 15)
ME12: S'ness 1B 52
Bridgeside M. ME15: Maid ...2H 43
Bridge St. ME15: Loose 7J 43
Bridgewater Pl. ME19: Leyb ...1F 35
Bridgewater Rd.
ME12: S'ness 4B 52
Brielle Way ME11: Queen ...6A 52
Brier Cl. ME5: Chat'm 1G 21
Brier Rd. ME10: Sit 4J 25
Bright Rd. ME4: Chat'm 6F 15
Brindle Way ME5: Lord W 1G 33
Brisbane Av. ME10: Sit 3A 28
Brisbane Rd.
ME4: Chat'm 7D 4 (5E 14)
Brishing Cl. ME15: Maid 7D 44
Brishing La. ME15: Maid 7D 44
ME17: Bou Mo 3C 50
Brishing Rd.
ME17: Bou Mo, Cha S ...1D 50

Brisley's Row ME1: Burh 1H 31
Brissenden Cl. ME2: Upnor ...4E 10
Bristol Cl. ME2: Strood 3F 13
Bristol Ho. ME15: Maid 5C 44
(off Northumberland Rd.)
Britannia Bus. Pk.
ME20: Aylfd 3B 36
Britannia Cl. ME2: Hall'g 5C 18
ME10: Sit 7C 26
Briton Cl. ME2: S'ness 3A 52
Britton St. ME7: Gill 4F 5 (3F 15)
(not continuous)
Broader La. ME14: Det 1F 39
Broadfield Rd. ME15: Maid ...4K 43
Broadlands ME5: W'slade 5F 21
Broadoak ME19: Leyb 1E 34
Broadoak Av. ME15: Maid ...4K 43
BROAD STREET 2F 11
Broad St. ME12: S'ness 2B 52
ME17: Sut V 6K 51
Broadview Av. ME8: Gill 1E 22
Broadwater Rd. ME19: W Mal ..6D 34
Broadway ME8: Gill 5A 16
ME12: S'ness 2C 52
ME16: Maid 5G 7 (1J 43)
Broadway, The ME14: Minst ...4H 53
Broadway Hgts. ME16: Maid ...5G 7
Broadway Shop. Cen.
ME16: Maid 4G 7 (7J 37)
Broadwood Rd. ME3: C'den ...3E 10
Brockbank Cl. ME5: W'slade ...1E 32
Brockenhurst Av. ME15: Maid ..3A 44
Brockenhurst Cl. ME8: Wigm ...2C 22
Brockman Pl. ME14: Maid ...3J 7
Brogden Cres. ME17: Leeds ...5A 46
Brogden Farm Cotts.
ME17: Leeds 5A 46
Bromley Cl. ME5: Lord W 5F 21
(not continuous)
ME9: N'tn 4C 24
BROMPTON 1E 14
Brompton Barracks 1E 14
Brompton Cl. ME4: Chat'm ...2D 14
Brompton Farm Rd.
ME2: Strood 6H 9
Brompton Hill
ME4: Chat'm 1C 4 (2D 14)
Brompton La. ME2: Strood 7J 9
Brompton Rd. ME7: Gill ...3F 5 (2F 15)
Bronington Cl. ME5: W'slade ...4E 20
Bronte Cl. ME3: Cli W 2A 10
ME20: Lark 7B 30
Brook, The
ME4: Chat'm 3C 4 (3D 14)
Brookbank Ho. ME4: Pen H ...3K 37
Brooker Cl. ME17: Bou Mo ...7C 44
Brooker's Pl. ME3: High'm 1E 8
Brookes Pl. ME9: N'tn 3D 24
Brookfield Av. ME20: Lark ...6C 30
Brookland Lake 3D 30
Brooklands Rd. ME20: Lark ...6C 30
Brook La. ME6: Snod 4B 30
Brooklyn Paddock
ME7: Gill 2J 5 (2H 15)
Brookmead Rd. ME3: Cli W ...2A 10
Brook Rd. ME20: Lark 6A 30
Brookside ME3: Hoo W 2J 11
ME12: Minst 3H 53
Brooks Pl. ME1: Maid ...3K 7 (7K 37)
Brook St. ME6: Snod 4B 30
Brook Theatre, The
Chatham 3C 4 (3D 14)
Broomcroft Rd. ME8: Rain ...6F 17
BROOMFIELD 7E 46
Broomfield Rd.
ME17: Broom, Kgswd ...7E 46
Broom Hill Rd. ME2: Strood ...7H 9
Broom Rd. ME10: Sit 2G 29
Broomshaw Rd.
ME16: Barm 1C 42
Browndens Rd. ME2: Hall'g ...5A 18
Brownelow Copse
ME5: W'slade 1E 32
Brownhill Cl. ME5: W'slade ...5E 20
Browning Cl. ME20: Lark 6B 30
Brown St. ME8: Rain 7E 16
Brucks, The ME18: W'bury ...5F 41
Bruges Ct. ME10: Kems'y 5D 26
Brunel M. ME4: Chat'm 1E 14
Brunell Cl. ME16: Maid 6G 37
Brunswick M. ME16: Maid ...6H 37
Brunswick St.
ME15: Maid 6J 7 (1K 43)

Brunswick St. E.—Charlbury Cl.

Brunswick St. E.
ME15: Maid 5K 7 (1K 43)
Brushwood Cl. ME15: Maid 6B 44
Bryant Cl. ME18: Nett 6D 40
Bryant Rd. ME2: Strood 7J 9
Bryant St. ME4: Chat'm 6C 4 (5E 14)
Buckingham Rd.
ME7: Gill 4K 5 (3H 15)
Buckingham Row
ME15: Maid 5D 44
Buckland Cl. ME5: W'slade 7E 20
Buckland Gdns. ME16: Maid 3F 7
Buckland Hill
ME16: Maid 2F 7 (6H 37)
Buckland Ho. *ME2: Strood 4G 13*
(off Whitehead Dr.)
Buckland La. ME16: Alltn 5G 37
(not continuous)
Buckland Pl.
ME16: Maid 3F 7 (7H 37)
(not continuous)
Buckland Ri.
ME16: Maid 2F 7 (6H 37)
Buckland Rd.
ME16: Alltn, Maid 2F 7 (6H 37)
Buckmore Pk. 6A 20
Buckmore Pk. Kart Circuit 5A 20
Buckthorne Rd. ME12: Minst 7G 53
Buddle Dr. ME12: Minst 5E 52
Buglehorn Cotts.
ME15: Otham 6G 45
Buhrstone Ho. *ME7: Gill 3G 5*
(off Mill Rd.)
Bulldog Rd. ME5: Lord W 7F 21
Buller Rd.
ME4: Chat'm 7C 4 (6D 14)
Bullfields ME6: Snod 2C 30
Bull La. ME1: Roch 4B 6 (2A 14)
ME3: High'm 1F 9
ME9: N'tn, S'bry 7A 24
ME20: Aylfd, Eccl 7H 31
Bull Orchard ME16: Barm 2C 42
Bulrush Cl. ME5: W'slade 6D 20
Bumbles Cl. ME1: Roch 2B 20
Bungalows, The
ME3: Hoo W 2H 11
Bunny Hill DA12: Shorne 5A 8
Bunters Hill Rd.
ME3: Cli W, Wain 2J 9
Burberry La. ME17: Leeds 7A 46
Burdett Av. DA12: Shorne 3A 8
Burdock Ct. ME16: Maid 1D 42
Burgess Cotts. ME17: Leeds 7A 46
Burgess Hall Dr. ME17: Leeds 6A 46
Burgess Rd.
ME2: Strood 1A 6 (1K 13)
Burghclere Dr. ME16: Maid 2E 42
Burgoyne Ct. ME14: Maid 4J 37
BURHAM 1H 31
BURHAM COMMON 7J 19
BURHAM COURT 1F 31
Burham Ct. ME1: Burh 1F 31
Burham Down (Nature Reserve)
1J 31
Burham Marsh Local Nature Reserve
2E 30
Burham Rd. ME1: Woul 2G 19
Burial Ground La.
ME15: Maid 2H 43
Burkston Cl. ME10: Kems'y 6E 26
Burleigh Cl. ME2: Strood 7G 9
Burleigh Dr. ME14: Maid 2J 37
Burley Rd. ME10: Sit 3C 28
Burlington Gdns. ME8: Parkw 5E 22
Burmarsh Cl. ME5: W'slade 4F 21
Burma Way ME5: Chat'm 3D 20
Burnham Cl. ME10: Sit 6C 26
Burnham Wlk. ME8: Parkw 6E 22
(not continuous)
Burn Mdw. Cotts. ME14: Boxl 7G 33
Burns Rd. ME7: Gill 1G 5 (1G 15)
ME16: Maid 3F 43
Burnt Ash Rd. ME20: Aylfd 3B 36
Burnt Ho. Cl. ME3: Wain 5A 10
Burnt Oak Ter.
ME7: Gill 2H 5 (2G 15)
Burnup Bank ME10: Sit 2G 29
Burritt M. ME1: Roch 5A 14
Burrs, The ME10: Sit 4D 28
Burrstock Way ME8: Rain 6H 17
Burston Rd. ME17: Cox 3E 48
Burton Cl. ME3: Wain 4A 10
Busbridge Cl. ME19: E Mal 4G 35
Busbridge Rd. ME6: Snod 3A 30
ME15: Loose 6H 43
Bushmeadow Rd. ME8: Rain 6F 17
Bush Rd. ME2: Cux 5A 12
Bush Row ME20: Aylfd 7J 31
Butchers Hill DA12: Shorne 4A 8
Butlers Pk. Way
ME2: Strood 4G 13
Buttercup Av. ME12: Minst 7H 53
Buttermere Cl. ME7: Gill 3K 15
Butt Grn. La. ME17: Lint 7J 49
Butt Haw Cl. ME3: Hoo W 2J 11
Button Ho. ME3: C'den 1C 10
Button La. ME15: Bear 2G 45
Butts, The ME10: Sit 3D 28
Buxton Cl. ME5: Lord W 1H 33
ME15: Maid 4K 43
Bychurch Pl.
ME15: Maid 6K 7 (1K 43)
Byron Rd. ME7: Gill 5G 15
ME14: Pen H 4A 38
Bythorne Ct. ME8: Rain 7H 17

C

Cades Pl. *ME16: Maid 7F 37*
(off Malling Ter.)
Cadnam Cl. ME2: Strood 7G 9
Caernarvon Dr. ME15: Maid 3J 43
Cagney Cl. ME3: Wain 5A 10
Caldecote Cl. ME8: Rain 7H 17
Calder Rd. ME14: Maid 4H 37
Caldew Av. ME8: Gill 7C 16
Caldew Gro. ME10: Sit 4F 29
Caledonian Ct. ME8: Gill 1E 22
Calehill Cl. ME14: Maid 5B 38
Callams Cl. ME8: Parkw 3D 22
Callaways La. ME9: N'tn 3D 24
Callisto Ct. ME16: Maid 1G 43
Callis Way ME8: Parkw 4D 22
Calthorpe M. ME2: Strood 7K 9
Camborne Mnr.
ME7: Gill 3G 5 (2G 15)
Cambria Av. ME1: Roch 6H 13
Cambridge Cres. ME15: Maid 5C 44
Cambridge Rd. ME2: Strood 7J 9
ME8: Wigm 3C 22
ME10: Sit 4F 29
Cambridge Ter.
ME4: Chat'm 4B 4 (4D 14)
Cambridge Way ME15: Maid 5C 44
Camden Cl. ME5: Lord W 4F 21
Camden Rd. ME7: Gill 1J 5 (1H 15)
Camden St.
ME14: Maid 2J 7 (6K 37)
Camelia Rd. ME12: Minst 7H 53
Camellia Cl. ME8: Wigm 2D 22
Cameron Cl. ME5: Chat'm 1F 21
Camomile Dr. ME14: Weav 6E 38
Campbell Rd.
ME15: Maid 6J 7 (1K 43)
Camperdown Mnr. *ME7: Gill 2E 14*
(off River St.)
Campion Cl. ME5: W'slade 6C 20
Campleshon Rd. ME8: Parkw 4D 22
Campus Way ME8: Gill 1A 22
Camp Way ME15: Maid 5B 44
Canada Ter. ME14: Maid 4K 37
Canadian Av. ME7: Gill 4J 15
Canal Rd. ME2: Strood 2B 6 (1A 14)
ME3: High'm 1E 8
Canberra Gdns. ME10: Sit 3A 28
Canning St. ME14: Maid 5K 37
Canon Cl. ME1: Roch 6K 13
Canon La. ME18: W'bury 2D 40
Canterbury Christ Church University
Medway Campus 7F 11
(off Pembroke)
Canterbury Ct. *ME10: Sit 4E 28*
(off Canterbury Rd.)
Canterbury Ho. ME15: Maid 5C 44
Canterbury La. ME8: Rain 6J 17
Canterbury Rd. ME10: Sit 4F 29
(not continuous)
Canterbury St.
ME7: Gill 4G 5 (3G 15)
Cantium Pl. ME6: Snod 1D 30
Cape Cotts. ME15: Loose 7J 43
Capel Cl. ME8: Parkw 4C 22
Capella ME1: Roch 7D 6
Capell Cl. ME17: Cox 3F 49
Capel Rd. ME10: Sit 4C 28
CAPSTONE 2J 21
Capstone Farm Country Pk. 3H 21
Capstone Farm Country Pk. Vis. Cen.
2H 21
Capstone Ridge ME7: Hpstd 4K 21
Capstone Rd. ME5: Chat'm 7G 15
ME7: Chat'm, Gill 1H 21
Captain's Cl. ME17: Sut V 7K 51
Cardens Rd. ME3: Cli W 1A 10
Cardinal Cl. ME12: Minst 5K 53
Cardinal Wlk.
ME19: Kings H 1D 40
Cardine Cl. ME10: Sit 7C 26
Carillon Cl. ME3: Hoo W 1J 11
CARING 4J 45
Caring Farm Cotts.
ME17: Leeds 3J 45
Caring La. ME14: Bear 4J 45
ME17: Leeds 4J 45
Caring Rd. ME17: Leeds 2H 45
Carisbrooke Dr. ME16: Maid 6G 37
Carisbrooke Rd.
ME2: Strood 6G 9
Carlisle Cl. ME2: Strood 2E 12
Carlisle Ho. ME15: Maid 5C 44
Carlton Av. ME7: Gill 7K 5 (4J 15)
ME12: S'ness 3B 52
Carlton Cl. ME19: Kings H 1C 40
Carlton Cres. ME5: Chat'm 1H 21
Carlton Gdns. ME15: Maid 4K 43
Carman's Cl. ME15: Loose 3H 49
Carnation Cl. ME19: E Mal 2H 35
Carnation Cres. ME10: Sit 6D 28
ME19: E Mal 3G 35
Carnation Rd. ME2: Strood 1F 13
Caroline Ct. ME15: Maid 5J 7
Caroline Cres. ME16: Alltn 4G 37
Carp Cl. ME20: Lark 6C 30
Carpeaux Cl.
ME4: Chat'm 5E 4 (4E 14)
Carpenters Cl. ME1: Roch 6C 14
Carpinus Cl. ME5: W'slade 1F 33
Carrie Ho. ME16: Maid 2F 7
Carrington Cl. ME7: Gill 2K 15
Carroll Cl. ME2: Hall'g 5C 18
Carroll Gdns. ME20: Lark 7B 30
Carton Cl. ME1: Roch 6B 14
Carton Rd. ME3: High'm 4D 8
Carvoran Way ME8: Wigm 4C 22
Casson Ct. ME4: Chat'm 1D 20
Castleacres Ind. Pk.
ME10: Sit 1F 29
Castle Av. ME1: Roch 4A 14
Castle Ct. ME11: Queen 7A 52
Castle Dene ME14: Maid 3H 37
Castle Hill ME1: Roch 4B 6 (2A 14)
ME14: T'hm 3J 39
Castle Hill Ct. ME1: Roch 4B 6
Castlemaine Av. ME7: Gill 2K 15
Castlemere Av. ME11: Queen 7B 52
Castle Rd. ME4: Chat'm 6E 14
ME10: Sit 3E 28
(not continuous)
ME16: Alltn 2G 37
Castle Rd. Bus. Pct.
ME10: Sit 1F 29
Castle Rd. Technology Cen.
ME10: Sit 2F 29
Castle Rough La.
ME10: Kems'y 5D 26
Castle St. ME1: Woul 5E 18
ME2: Upnor 6C 10
ME11: Queen 7A 52
Castle Vw. ME14: Maid 3H 37
Castle Vw. Bus. Cen.
ME1: Roch 3D 6 (2B 14)
Castle Vw. Mews ME1: Roch 4B 6
Castle Vw. Rd. ME2: Strood 1J 13
Castle Way ME19: Leyb 2E 34
Catamaran Yacht Club 2F 53
Catherine Cl. ME16: Barm 1D 42
Catherine's Ct. ME1: Roch 6D 6
Catherine St. ME1: Roch 5B 14
Catkin Cl. ME5: W'slade 1D 32
Catlyn Cl. ME19: E Mal 3G 35
Catterick Rd. ME5: Lord W 7H 21
Catts All. ME6: Snod 3C 30
Caulkers Ho. *ME4: Chat'm 6F 15*
(off Shipwrights Av.)
Causeway, The ME4: St Mary 5F 11
Cave Hill ME15: Maid 3J 43
Cavell Way ME10: Sit 2B 28
Cavendish Av. ME7: Gill 2J 15
Cavendish Pl. ME15: Bear 1G 45
Cavendish Rd. ME1: Roch 5B 14
Cavendish Way ME15: Bear 1F 45
Caversham Cl. ME8: Rain 7F 17
Cavour Rd. ME12: S'ness 2C 52
Cazeneuve St.
ME1: Roch 6C 6 (3A 14)
Cecil Av. ME2: Strood 7K 9
ME8: Gill 6A 16
ME12: S'ness 3B 52
Cecil Rd. ME1: Roch 5A 14
Cedar Cl. ME10: Sit 5F 29
ME20: Dit 3A 36
Cedar Ct. ME14: Maid 6A 38
Cedar Dr. ME16: Barm 2B 42
Cedar Gro. ME7: Hpstd 4A 22
Cedar Ho. *ME12: S'ness 2B 52*
(off Russell St.)
Cedar Rd. ME2: Strood 2G 13
ME3: Hoo W 4J 11
Cedars, The ME10: Sit 2G 29
Cedarwood ME16: Maid 6G 37
Celestine Cl. ME5: W'slade 1E 32
Cellini Wlk. ME19: Kings H 2D 40
Celt Cl. ME10: Kems'y 6D 26
Cemetery Cotts. ME15: Maid 5B 44
Cemetery Rd. ME2: Hall'g 5C 18
ME6: Snod 1B 30
Central Av. ME4: Chat'm 7F 11
ME10: Sit 4D 28
Central Bus. Pk. ME2: Med E 1C 14
Central Pde. ME1: Roch 6B 14
Central Pk. Gdns.
ME4: Chat'm 6C 14
Central Pk. Greyhound Stadium
1G 29
Central Rd. ME2: Strood 1J 13
ME20: Lark 7D 30
Central Ter. ME3: C'den 1D 10
Central Theatre
Chatham 4C 4 (4D 14)
Centre 2000 ME10: Sit 3E 28
Centre Ct. ME2: Med E 1C 14
Centurion Cl. ME8: Gill 7K 15
Century Ct. ME1: Roch 5C 6
Century M. ME1: Roch 5C 6
Century Rd. ME8: Gill 1D 22
Ceres Ct. ME10: Sit 2G 29
Chada Av. ME7: Gill 5J 15
Chaffe's La. ME9: Upc 6K 17
Chaffinch Cl. ME5: Chat'm 2E 20
Chalfont Dr. ME8: Gill 3D 22
Chalgrove M. ME2: Hall'g 4C 18
Chalkenden Av. ME8: Gill 6A 16
Chalkhill Cl. ME9: Iwade 3B 26
Chalk Pit Hill
ME4: Chat'm 7D 4 (5E 14)
Chalk Rd. ME3: High'm 1E 8
ME11: Queen 7A 52
CHALKWELL 2A 28
Chalkwell Rd. ME10: Sit 3B 28
Chalky Bank Rd. ME8: Rain 6F 17
Challenger Cl. ME10: Sit 7C 26
Challock Wlk. ME14: Maid 5B 38
Chalmers Way ME8: Gill 4A 16
Chamberlain Av. ME16: Maid 2E 42
Chamberlain Ct. ME8: Wigm 4B 22
Chamberlain Rd.
ME4: Chat'm 6F 15
Chancery La.
ME15: Maid 4K 7 (1A 44)
Chandlers Wharf
ME1: Roch 6A 6 (3K 13)
Chapel Cotts. ME17: Leeds 7A 46
Chapel La. ME2: Hall'g 5A 18
ME7: Hpstd 5A 22
(not continuous)
ME14: Bear 6F 39
Chapel Pk. ME10: Sit 1G 29
Chapel Rd. ME6: Snod 2C 30
ME17: Sut V 6K 51
Chapel St. ME12: Minst 6K 53
ME12: S'ness 1A 52
ME19: E Mal 5H 35
Chaplin Cl. ME3: Wain 4A 10
Chapman Av. ME15: Maid 3D 44
Chapman Way ME19: E Mal 3G 35
Chappell Way ME10: Sit 1B 28
Chapter Rd. ME2: Strood 1H 13
Chard Ho. ME14: Maid 4J 37
Charing Rd. ME8: Gill 5B 16
Chariot Way ME2: Strood 5G 13
Charlbury Cl. ME16: Maid 1F 43

58 A-Z Maidstone & Medway Towns

Charlecote Ct. *ME8: Gill* 1D 22
(off Derwent Way)
Charles Busby Ct.
ME20: Aylfd 2C 36
Charles Dickens Av.
ME3: High'm 5E 8
Charles Dr. *ME2: Cux* 5D 12
Charles St. *ME2: Strood* ...1J 13
ME4: Chat'm 6A 4 (5C 14)
ME12: S'ness 1A 52
ME16: Maid 6F 7 (1H 43)
Charleworth Ho.
ME4: Chat'm 6C 14
Charlock Cl. *ME16: Alltn* ...3G 37
Charlock Dr. *ME12: Minst* ...7G 53
Charlotte Cl. *ME5: W'slade* ...3F 21
Charlotte Dr. *ME8: Gill* 7C 16
ME19: Kings H 1E 40
Charlotte St. *ME10: Sit* 2C 28
Charlton La. *ME15: W Far* ...5A 42
Charlton Mnr. *ME7: Gill* ..4F 5 (3G 15)
Charlton St. *ME16: Maid* 2F 43
CHART CORNER 4G 51
Chart Cnr. *ME17: Cha S* 4G 51
Charter St.
ME4: Chat'm 7C 4 (6D 14)
ME7: Gill 1G 5 (1G 15)
CHART HILL 6G 51
Chart Hill Rd.
ME17: Bou Mo, Cha S 7E 50
Chart Pl. *ME8: Parkw* 6C 22
Chart Rd. *ME17: Cha S, Sut V* ...6G 51
CHART SUTTON 4G 51
Chart Sutton Bus. Est.
ME17: Cha S 3G 51
Chartway St.
ME17: Sut V, Kgswd 4K 51
Chartwell Ct.
ME4: Chat'm 5A 4 (4C 14)
ME7: Gill 5H 5 (3H 15)
Chartwell Dr. *ME16: Maid* ...7E 36
Chartwell Gro. *ME10: Sit* 4A 28
Chase, The *ME4: Chat'm* 6B 14
ME8: Gill 6A 16
Chatfield Way *ME19: E Mal* ...2J 35
CHATHAM 4C 4 (4D 14)
Chatham Docks *ME4: Chat'm* ...7F 11
Chatham Garrison ...1E 4 (2E 14)
Chatham Golf Cen. 1F 21
Chatham Gro. *ME4: Chat'm* ...7D 14
Chatham Hill *ME5: Chat'm* 5F 15
ME7: Gill 5F 15
CHATHAM MARITIME 6F 11
Chatham Rd. *ME5: Blue H* ...1B 32
ME14: Maid 4J 37
ME14: S'Ing 2B 32
ME20: Aylfd 2B 32
Chatham Ski & Snowboard Cen.
...............3J 21
Chatham Station (Rail)
...........5B 4 (4D 14)
Chatsworth Dr. *ME2: Strood* ...6K 9
ME10: Sit 4K 25
Chatsworth Rd.
ME7: Gill 2H 5 (2G 15)
CHATTENDEN 3D 10
Chattenden Cl. *ME14: Pen H* ...4A 38
Chattenden La. *ME3: C'den* ...2D 10
Chattenden Ter. *ME3: C'den* ...2D 10
Chaucer Cl. *ME2: Med E* 7C 10
ME15: Maid 5D 44
Chaucer Rd. *ME7: Gill* 5H 15
ME10: Sit 4B 28
Chaucer Way *ME20: Lark* 6B 30
Chavasse Ter. *ME5: Chat'm* ...2E 20
Chegwell Dr. *ME5: W'slade* ...5F 21
CHEGWORTH 6H 47
Chegworth Gdns. *ME10: Sit* ...6B 28
Chegworth La. *ME17: H'shm* ...6G 47
Chegworth Mill Cotts.
ME17: H'shm 6H 47
Chegworth Rd. *ME17: H'shm* ...5G 47
Chelmar Rd. *ME4: Chat'm* ...4F 15
Chelmsford Cl. *ME15: Maid* ...6D 44
Chelmsford Rd. *ME2: Strood* ...2F 13
Chelsfield Ho. *ME16: Maid* ...6G 37
Cheltenham Cl. *ME15: Maid* ...6E 44
Cheney Cl. *ME8: Parkw* 4D 22
Chenies, The
ME15: Maid 4K 51 (7A 38)

Chepstow Ho. *ME15: Maid* ...6E 44
Chequers Cl. *ME5: W'slade* ...2E 32
Chequers Ct. *ME2: Strood* ...6J 9
ME3: High'm 1E 8
Chequers Rd. *ME12: Minst* ...6K 53
CHEQUERS STREET 1F 9
Chequers St. *ME3: High'm* ...1E 8
Cherbourg Cres. *ME5: Chat'm* ...2D 20
Cheriton Rd. *ME8: Gill* 1D 22
Cheriton Way *ME16: Alltn* ...4F 37
Cherries, The *ME16: Barm* ...2C 42
Cherry Amber Cl. *ME8: Rain* ...1F 23
Cherry Cl. *ME10: Sit* 1B 28
Cherryfields *ME10: Sit* 4J 25
Cherry Hill Ct. *ME9: N'tn* ...3D 24
CHERRY ORCHARD 1E 42
Cherry Orchard *ME20: Dit* ...3K 35
Cherry Orchard Way
ME16: Maid 1E 42
Cherry Rd. *ME3: Hoo W* 4J 11
Cherry Tree Cl. *ME12: S'ness* ...4A 52
Cherry-Tree Pk.
ME17: Bou Mo 3A 50
Cherry Tree Rd. *ME8: Rain* ...1F 23
Cherry Vw. *ME17: Bou Mo* ...2A 50
Chervilles *ME16: Barm* 2D 42
Chesham Dr. *ME8: Gill* 3E 22
Cheshire Rd. *ME15: Maid* ...5D 44
(Lichfield Ho.)
ME15: Maid 1D 44
(Mansion Cotts.)
CHESLEY 6C 24
Chester Cl. *ME2: Strood* 2F 13
Chester Rd. *ME7: Gill* 6H 15
Chesterton Rd. *ME20: Lark* ...6B 30
Chestfield Cl. *ME8: Rain* 6E 16
Chestnut Av. *ME5: W'slade* ...6C 20
Chestnut Cl. *ME15: Maid* 1E 50
ME19: Kings H 2B 40
Chestnut Dr. *ME17: Cox* 2E 48
Chestnut Rd. *ME2: Strood* ...2G 13
CHESTNUT STREET 5G 25
Chestnut St. *ME9: B'den* ...5G 25
Chestnut Wlk. *ME20: Lark* ...1J 35
Chestnut Wood La.
ME9: B'den 6G 25
Chetney Cl. *ME2: Strood* 1E 12
Chetney Vw. *ME9: Iwade* ...2A 26
Chevening Cl. *ME5: W'slade* ...4E 20
Cheviot Gdns. *ME15: Bear* ...3F 45
Cheyne Cl. *ME10: Kems'y* ...6D 26
Chicago Av. *ME7: Gill* 3J 15
Chichester Cl. *ME8: Rain* 1G 23
Chickfield Gdns. *ME5: Chat'm* ...6G 15
Chiddingfold Cl. *ME12: Minst* ...6K 53
Chiddingstone Cl.
ME15: Maid 6E 44
Chieftain Cl. *ME8: Gill* 7B 16
Childscroft Rd. *ME8: Rain* ...6F 17
Chilham Cl.
ME4: Chat'm 6A 4 (5C 14)
ME12: S'ness 4B 52
Chilham Ho. *ME2: Strood* ...6A 10
Chilham Rd. *ME8: Gill* 5A 16
ME16: Alltn 4F 37
Chillington Cl. *ME2: Hall'g* ...5A 18
Chillington St. *ME14: Maid* ...5J 37
Chiltern Cl. *ME15: Bear* 3E 44
Chiltern Pl. *ME14: Det* 2F 39
Chilton Av. *ME10: Sit* 4D 28
Chilton Cl. *ME8: Rain* 7E 16
Chilton Dr. *ME3: High'm* 4D 8
CHILTON HILLS 3D 8
Chimes, The *ME1: Roch* 6C 6
ME3: Hoo W 1J 11
ME14: Bear 6F 39
Chippendale Cl.
ME5: W'slade 1D 32
Chipstead Cl. *ME16: Alltn* ...5G 37
Chipstead Rd. *ME8: Parkw* ...5D 22
Chislehurst Cl. *ME15: Maid* ...6E 44
Chislet Wlk. *ME8: Rain* 6F 17
Chorister Cres. *ME3: Hoo W* ...1J 11
Christchurch Ct. *ME5: Chat'm* ...7G 15
(off Luton High St.)
Christchurch Ho. *ME15: Maid* ...7D 44
Christen Way *ME15: Maid* ...6C 44
Christie Cl. *ME5: W'slade* ...3F 21
Christie Dr. *ME20: Lark* 6B 30
Christmas St. *ME7: Gill* 1J 15
Christopher Rd.
ME4: Chat'm 7E 4 (6E 14)

Church Farm Cl. *ME3: Hoo W* ...3J 11
Church Fld. *ME6: Snod* 1D 30
Church Flds. *ME19: W Mal* ...3C 34
Churchfields Ter.
ME1: Roch 7A 6 (4K 13)
Church Grn. *ME2: Strood* ...7A 10
Church Hill *ME15: Chat'm* ...6G 15
ME17: Bou Mo 3A 50
Church M. *ME5: Chat'm* 3D 20
Churchill Cotts.
ME17: Leeds 6A 46
Churchill Ho. *ME10: Sit* 2F 29
ME16: Maid 2E 42
Churchill Rd. *ME12: Minst* ...6K 53
Churchill Sq. *ME19: Kings H* ...1B 40
Churchlands *ME4: Chat'm* ...7D 14
ME14: Maid 1K 7
Church La. *ME4: Chat'm* 2D 14
ME9: N'tn 3D 24
ME14: Bear 7H 39
ME15: W Far 5A 42
ME16: Barm 3B 42
Church M. *ME6: Snod* 2C 30
ME8: Rain 1F 23
ME9: Iwade 2C 26
Church Path
ME2: Strood 1A 6 (1K 13)
ME7: Gill 2K 5 (2H 15)
(Parr Av.)
ME7: Gill 2F 5 (2F 15)
(Prince Arthur Rd.)
Church Pl. *ME1: Woul* 4E 18
Church Rd. *ME9: Tonge* 3J 29
ME10: Sit 3F 29
ME15: Maid 7F 7 (2H 43)
ME15: Otham, Bear 4E 44
ME17: Cha S 5H 51
ME19: Rya 1A 34
Church Rd. Bus. Cen.
................1F 29
Church Row *ME6: Snod* 3C 30
ME1: Burh 2G 31
ME1: Roch 7D 6 (4B 14)
ME3: High'm 1E 8
ME3: Hoo W 2J 11
ME4: Chat'm 5D 4 (5E 14)
(not continuous)
ME7: Gill 2J 15
ME9: Rod 7G 29
ME10: Sit 3C 28
(Dover St.)
ME10: Sit 1F 29
(St Paul's St.)
ME14: Maid 3J 7 (7K 37)
ME15: Loose 7J 43
ME15: Maid 7F 7 (2H 43)
ME17: Bou Mo 5H 49
ME18: Tstn 5H 41
Church Ter. *ME5: Chat'm* ...6G 15
Church Wlk. *ME19: E Mal* ...4H 35
ME20: Aylfd 7H 31
Chute Cl. *ME8: Parkw* 5D 22
Cineworld Cinema
Rochester 5G 13
Cinnabar Cl. *ME5: W'slade* ...1E 32
Cinnabar Dr. *ME10: Sit* 1A 28
Cinnamon Gro. *ME16: Maid* ...1D 42
City Way *ME1: Roch* 7D 6 (4B 14)
Claire Ho. *ME16: Maid* ...2F 7 (6H 37)
Clandon Rd. *ME5: Lord W* ...7H 21
Clare La. *ME19: E Mal* 3F 35
Claremont Rd. *ME14: Maid* ...6A 38
Claremont Way
ME4: Chat'm 5C 4 (5D 14)
Clarence Av. *ME1: Roch* 4A 14
Clarence St. *ME14: Weav* ...7D 38
Clarence Rd. *ME4: Chat'm* ...6F 15
Clarence Row *ME12: S'ness* ...2C 52
Clarence Twr.
ME1: Roch 7A 6 (4K 13)
Clarendon Cl. *ME10: Sit* 6D 28
ME14: Bear 7F 39
Clarendon Dr. *ME2: Strood* ...6J 9
Clarendon Pl. *ME14: Maid* ...3K 7
Clare Pl. *ME15: Maid* 6C 44
Clare Way *ME15: Maid* 6C 44
Clare Wood Dr. *ME19: E Mal* ...3F 35
Claridge Ct. *ME7: Hpstd* ...5K 21
Clare Farm Ct. *ME12: Minst* ...6F 53
Clark M. *ME20: Aylfd* 2C 36
Clavell Cl. *ME8: Parkw* 5E 22
Claxfield Rd. *ME9: Lyn, Tey* ...7K 29

Claygate *ME15: Maid* 3C 44
ME17: Holl 2E 46
Clearheart La. *ME19: Kings H* ...1E 40
Cleave Rd. *ME7: Gill* 6J 15
Cleeve Ct. *ME19: Kings H* ...2C 40
Clematis Av. *ME8: Wigm* 4B 22
Clemens Pl. *ME19: Kings H* ...2D 40
Clement Cl. *ME10: Sit* 6C 26
Clement Cl. *ME16: Maid* 6G 37
Clerke Dr. *ME10: Kems'y* ...6E 26
Clermont Cl. *ME7: Hpstd* ...6A 22
Cleveland Ho. *ME16: Maid* ...2E 42
Cleveland Rd.
ME7: Gill 2K 5 (2H 15)
Clewson Ri. *ME14: Pen H* ...3A 38
Cliffe Ct. *ME2: Med E* 7C 10
Cliffe Rd. *ME2: Strood* ...1A 6 (5J 9)
CLIFFE WOODS 1A 10
Cliff Gdns. *ME17: Maid* 6K 53
Cliff Hill *ME17: Bou Mo* ...1B 50
Cliff Hill Rd. *ME17: Bou Mo* ...1B 50
Cliffhouse Av. *ME12: Minst* ...5K 53
Clifford Cres. *ME10: Sit* 3H 29
Clifford Way
ME16: Maid 7F 7 (2H 43)
Clifton Cl. *ME2: Strood* 1H 13
ME14: Maid 6A 38
Clifton Rd. *ME7: Gill* ...1H 5 (1H 15)
Clinton Av. *ME2: Strood* 7F 9
Clinton Cl. *ME17: Cox* 2E 48
Clipper Cl. *ME2: Med E* 1C 14
Clipper Ct. *ME2: Med E* 1C 14
Cliveden Cl. *ME16: Alltn* ...4G 37
Clive Ho. *ME20: Aylfd* 3C 36
Clive Rd. *ME1: Roch* 5A 14
ME10: Sit 4K 25
Clockhouse Ri. *ME17: Cox* ...3F 49
Clock Twr. M. *ME16: Maid* ...1C 30
Cloisterham Rd. *ME1: Roch* ...2B 20
Cloisters, The *ME10: Sit* ...3C 28
Clopton Cl. *ME8: Gill* 1D 22
Close, The *ME1: Roch* ...7B 6 (4A 14)
Cloudberry Cl. *ME16: Alltn* ...5G 37
Cloudesley Cl. *ME1: Roch* ...7K 13
Clovelly Dr. *ME12: Minst* ...4H 53
Clover Bank Vw.
ME5: Chat'm 3F 21
Clover Cl. *ME12: Minst* 7G 53
Clover Cl. *ME10: Sit* 2F 29
Clover Lay *ME8: Rain* 6G 17
Cloverlay Ind. Pk. *ME8: Rain* ...7H 17
Clover Rd. *ME3: Hoo W* 4J 11
Clover St.
ME4: Chat'm 5C 4 (4D 14)
(not continuous)
Clover Ter. *ME15: Maid* 4C 44
Cluxton Rd. Industries
ME15: Maid 7E 44
Clyde St. *ME12: S'ness* 2D 52
Coachman's M.
ME1: Roch 5C 6 (3A 14)
Coach Yard, The *ME16: Maid* ...1E 42
Coats Av. *ME12: S'ness* 4A 52
Cobb Cl. *ME2: Strood* 7F 9
Cobbett Cl. *ME19: E Mal* ...3G 35
Cobblestones *ME7: Hpstd* ...4K 21
Cobbs Cl. *ME18: W'bury* 5F 41
Cobden Rd. *ME4: Chat'm* 6F 15
Cobdown Cl. *ME20: Dit* 1J 35
Cobdown Gro. *ME8: Rain* ...6G 17
Cobdown Pk. *ME20: Dit* 1K 35
Cob Dr. *DA12: Shorne* 4A 8
Cobfields *ME17: Cha S* 4F 51
Cobham Av. *ME10: Sit* 6C 28
Cobham Cl. *ME2: Strood* 1G 13
ME16: Maid 7H 37
Cobham Dr. *ME19: Kings H* ...1D 40
Cobham Ri. *ME7: Gill* 3J 15
Cobnut Cl. *ME14: Weav* 7C 38
Cobtree Cl. *ME5: Chat'm* ...1G 21
Cobtree Manor Pk. 1G 37
Cobtree Manor Pk. Golf Course
.................7C 32
Cobtree Rd. *ME17: Cox* 2F 49
Cobtree Rdbt. *ME5: S'Ing* ...1H 37
Cockham Cotts. *ME3: Hoo W* ...3H 11
COCK STREET 3C 50
Coe's Grn. *ME3: C'den* 3E 10
Colchester Cl. *ME5: Chat'm* ...2D 20
Coldblow Cotts.
ME17: Bou Mo 3K 49
Coldblow La. *ME14: T'hm* ...4K 39
COLD HARBOUR 3H 25

Cold Harbour La.—Cutbush & Corrall Ct.

Cold Harbour La. ME9: Bob 3H 25
Coldharbour La.
ME10: Kems'y 5D 26
ME20: Aylfd 3D 36
Coldred Rd. ME15: Maid 1E 50
Colegate Dr. ME14: Bear 7H 39
Coleman Dr. ME10: Kems'y 5D 26
Coleridge Cl. ME20: Lark 6C 30
Coleshall Cl. ME15: Maid 6E 44
Coleshall Cotts. ME9: Iwade 3B 26
Colewood Dr. ME2: Strood 7D 8
Colfe Way ME10: Kems'y 6E 26
College Av. ME7: Gill 6F 5 (4F 15)
ME15: Maid 7H 7 (2J 43)
College Cotts.
ME15: Maid 6H 7 (1J 43)
College Ct.
ME15: Maid 6J 7 (1K 43)
College Rd. ME4: Chat'm 1D 14
ME10: Sit 5B 28
(not continuous)
ME15: Maid 5J 7 (1K 43)
ME20: Lark 7D 30
College Wlk.
ME15: Maid 6J 7 (1K 43)
College Yd. ME1: Roch 4C 6 (2A 14)
Collet Wlk. ME8: Parkw 5D 22
Collinge Cl. ME19: E Mal 2H 35
Collings Wlk. ME8: Parkw 5D 22
Collington Ter. ME15: Maid 1D 50
Collingwood Ind. Cen.
ME17: Sut V 3K 51
Collingwood Rd. ME20: Aylfd 3A 32
Collingwood Wlk. ME10: Sit 3K 25
Collis St. ME2: Strood 7J 9
Colman Pde.
ME14: Maid 3J 7 (7K 37)
Colson Dr. ME9: Iwade 3B 26
Coltsfoot Dr. ME14: Weav 7E 38
Columbine Cl. ME2: Strood 1G 13
ME19: E Mal 2G 35
Columbine Rd. ME2: Strood 1G 13
ME19: E Mal 2G 35
Combined Court Cen.
Maidstone 5H 7 (1J 43)
Command Rd. ME14: Maid 3J 37
Commercial Rd.
ME2: Strood 2A 6 (1J 13)
Commissioners Ct.
ME4: Chat'm 1C 4 (2D 14)
Commissioners Rd.
ME2: Med E, Strood
1C 6 (7A 10)
Commodore Rd. ME14: Maid 6B 38
Common, The
ME1: Roch 3C 6 (2A 14)
Common Rd. ME3: Cli W 2K 9
ME5: Blue H, Chat'm 6J 19
Commonwealth Cl. ME10: Sit 4F 29
Communications Pk.
ME2: Strood 3J 13
Compass Cen. ME4: Chat'm 7F 11
Compass Cl. ME1: Roch 7A 14
Compton Cl. ME5: Lord W 7H 21
Concord Av. ME5: Chat'm 4C 20
Coney M. ME4: Chat'm 7E 14
Conifer Dr. ME5: Lord W 1H 33
Coniston Cl. ME7: Gill 2A 16
Coniston Ho. ME15: Maid 5D 44
Connaught Cl. ME15: Maid 1E 50
Connaught M. ME4: Chat'm 6G 15
Connaught Rd. ME4: Chat'm 6F 15
ME7: Gill 4J 5 (3H 15)
ME10: Sit 4C 28
Conqueror Ct. ME10: Sit 3K 25
Conqueror Dr. ME7: Gill 2A 16
Conquest Ind. Est.
ME2: Strood 2J 13
Conrad Cl. ME8: Parkw 5D 22
(not continuous)
Consort Cl. ME14: Maid 6A 38
Consort Ho. ME2: Strood 1A 6
Constitution Hill ME5: Chat'm 5F 15
ME6: Snod 2B 30
Constitution Rd. ME5: Chat'm 5F 15
Contessa Cl. ME19: Kings H 7E 34
Conway Cl. ME2: Strood 6G 9
Conway M. ME7: Gill 1D 4 (2E 14)
Conway Rd. ME16: Alltn 5F 37
Conyers Wlk. ME8: Parkw 5D 22
Cooden Cl. ME8: Rain 6G 17
Cook Cl. ME5: Lord W 3G 21
Cookham Hill ME1: Roch 6J 13
Cookham Wood Rd.
ME1: Roch 1K 19
Cooks Cotts. ME18: W'bury 5D 40
Cook's La. ME10: Sit 1C 28
Cooks Wharf ME1: Roch 4C 14
Cooling Cl. ME14: Maid 5B 38
Cooling Comn. ME3: Cliffe 1B 10
Cooling Rd. ME2: Strood 5K 9
Coombe Cl. ME5: Lord W 6F 21
ME6: Snod 3C 30
Coombe Dr. ME10: Sit 4F 29
Coombe Rd. ME3: Hoo W 2J 11
ME15: Maid 7H 7 (2J 43)
Cooper Rd. ME5: Lord W 6E 20
ME6: Snod 4B 30
Copenhagen Rd.
ME7: Gill 5G 5 (3G 15)
Copland Av. ME12: Minst 6J 53
Copper Beech Cl. ME10: Sit 3B 28
Copperfield Cres. ME3: High'm 5E 8
Copperfield Dr. ME17: L'ly 1K 51
Copperfield Ho.
ME4: Chat'm 5C 4 (4D 14)
Copperfield Rd. ME1: Roch 6A 14
Copperfields, The
ME1: Roch 7A 6 (4K 13)
Coppergate ME7: Hpstd 3K 21
Copperhouse La. ME7: Gill 2B 16
Copperhouse Rd.
ME2: Strood 1E 12
Copperpenny Dr. ME7: Hpstd 6B 22
Copper Tree Ct. ME15: Maid 7K 43
Coppertree Wlk.
ME5: Lord W 1G 33
Coppice, The ME20: Aylfd 2B 36
Coppice Ct. ME7: Hpstd 5B 22
Coppice Rd. ME5: Lord W 7G 21
Coppice Vw. ME14: Weav 5D 38
Coppins La. ME9: B'den 7K 25
Copse, The ME3: Hoo W 4J 11
Copse Cl. ME1: Roch 7C 14
Copse Farm ME3: C'den 2D 10
Copsehill ME19: Leyb 1F 35
Copsewood Way ME15: Bear 1F 45
Coral Pk. ME14: Maid 6A 38
Coral Rd. ME12: Minst 7H 53
Corben Cl. ME16: Alltn 5D 36
Cordelia Cres. ME1: Roch 6H 13
Coriander Dr. ME16: Maid 1D 42
Cork St. ME20: Eccl 4H 31
Corkwell St.
ME4: Chat'm 7A 4 (5C 14)
Cormorant Cl. ME2: Strood 1E 12
Cormorant Rd. ME9: Iwade 3C 26
Cornflower Cl. ME14: Weav 7D 38
Cornflower Way ME12: Minst 7H 53
Cornhill Pl.
ME15: Maid 7G 7 (2J 43)
Cornwall Cl. ME15: Maid 5D 44
Cornwall Cres. ME1: Woul 5F 19
Cornwallis Av. ME4: Chat'm 7C 14
ME7: Gill 4K 15
ME17: Lint 5H 49
Cornwallis Cotts. ME17: Lint 3H 49
Cornwallis Rd. ME16: Maid 7G 37
Cornwallis Rdbt. ME7: Gill 4A 16
Cornwall Rd. ME1: Roch 5A 14
ME7: Gill 2H 5 (2H 15)
Corona Ter. ME6: Snod 4B 30
Coronation Cotts. ME9: Rod 6H 29
Coronation Cres.
ME11: Queen 7A 52
Coronation Flats
ME4: Chat'm 6C 4 (5D 14)
Coronation Rd. ME5: Chat'm 6G 15
ME12: S'ness 3C 52
Corporation Cotts.
ME20: Aylfd 7G 31
Corporation Rd.
ME7: Gill 2K 5 (2H 15)
Corporation St.
ME1: Roch 3C 6 (2A 14)
Corral Cl. ME5: Chat'm 6H 15
Corrall Almshouses
ME15: Maid 6J 7 (1K 43)
Corrance Grn. ME15: Maid 4K 43
Cortland Cl. ME10: Sit 1C 28
Cortland M. ME10: Sit 1C 28
Cory's Rd. ME1: Roch 3C 6 (2A 14)
Cossack St. ME1: Roch 5A 14
Cossington Rd. ME5: W'slade 2E 32
Cotswold Gdns. ME15: Bear 3F 45
Cottage Ind. Est. ME20: Aylfd 1E 36
Cottage Rd.
ME4: Chat'm 1C 4 (2D 14)
Cottall Av. ME4: Chat'm 6D 14
Cottenham Cl. ME19: E Mal 4G 35
Cotton Thistle Way
ME12: Minst 7H 53
Coulman St. ME7: Gill 5K 5 (3H 15)
Coulters Cl. ME14: Weav 7C 38
Council Cotts. ME15: E Far 1D 48
(not continuous)
County Court
Medway 3A 4 (3C 14)
County Ga.
ME14: Maid 1H 7 (6J 37)
County Gro. ME19: W Mal 3C 34
County Rd. ME14: Maid 2J 7 (6K 37)
Court Dr. ME16: Maid 7G 37
Courtenay Rd.
ME15: Maid 7G 7 (2J 43)
Courteney Rd. ME8: Gill 2B 22
Courtfield Av. ME5: Lord W 6F 21
Courtlands ME18: Tstn 4H 41
Courtlands Cl. ME18: Tstn 4H 41
Court Lodge DA12: Shorne 5A 8
Court Lodge Cotts.
ME15: E Far 5D 42
Court Lodge Farm
ME18: Tstn 5J 41
Court Lodge Rd. ME7: Gill 2K 15
ME17: H'shm 4K 47
Court Mdw. ME8: Gill 6B 16
Court Rd. ME1: Burh 1F 31
ME8: Rain 1G 23
ME10: Sit 7D 26
Courtyard, The ME8: Gill 1A 22
Coutts Av. DA12: Shorne 3A 8
Coventry Cl. ME2: Strood 2F 13
Coventry Ho. ME15: Maid 5C 44
Coverdale Av. ME15: Maid 6C 44
Coverdale Cl. ME5: Chat'm 2F 21
Covert, The ME5: W'slade 1E 32
Covey Hall Rd. ME6: Snod 1C 30
Cowbeck Cl. ME8: Parkw 3D 22
Cowden Rd. ME14: Maid 6B 38
Cowdrey Cl. ME1: Roch 6K 13
ME16: Maid 3E 42
Cowper Rd. ME7: Gill 5H 15
ME10: Sit 3F 29
Cowstead La. ME8: Rain 4E 16
Cowstead Rd. ME9: S'bry 6K 23
Cox Gdns. ME8: Gill 6A 16
COXHEATH 2F 49
Cox's Cl. ME6: Snod 2B 30
Cox St. ME9: Det 7F 23
Cozenton Cl. ME8: Rain 7E 16
Crabtree Cl. ME19: Kings H 2B 40
Crabtree Rd. ME8: Gill 1D 22
Craddock Way ME8: Parkw 4D 22
Cradles Rd. ME9: H'lip, S'bry 7J 23
Cragie Wlk. ME8: Parkw 5E 22
Cranborne Av. ME15: Maid 4A 44
Cranbrook Cl. ME8: Gill 5C 16
ME15: Maid 5E 44
Cranbrook Dr. ME10: Sit 6B 28
Cranford Cl. ME8: Rain 7D 16
Cranleigh Gdns. ME4: Chat'm 5B 14
ME16: Alltn 4F 37
Cranmer Ct. ME15: Maid 4A 44
Cranmere Ct.
ME2: Strood 1B 6 (7A 10)
Crayford Cl. ME14: Maid 5B 38
Crematorium Cotts.
ME14: Weav 5C 38
Cremers Rd. ME10: Sit 2F 29
Crescent, The ME4: St Mary 6F 11
ME10: Kems'y 5D 26
ME12: Minst 3G 53
(Hazel Gro.)
ME12: Minst 6E 52
(Lowfield Rd.)
ME14: Maid 3J 37
Crescent Ho. ME2: Strood 2B 6
Crescent St. ME10: Sit 3D 28
Crescent Way ME5: Chat'm 4B 20
Cressey Ct.
ME4: Chat'm 5A 4 (4C 14)
Crest Rd. ME1: Roch 7A 14
Crestway ME5: Chat'm 1F 21
Creve Coeur Cl. ME14: Weav 6F 39
Cricketers Cl. ME10: Kems'y 5D 26
ME17: H'shm 6K 47
Cripple St. ME15: Maid 4J 43
Crismill Cotts. ME14: Bear 1K 45
Crismill La.
ME14: Bear, T'hm
1K 45, 7K 39 & 1A 46
(not continuous)
Crispe Cl. ME8: Parkw 5D 22
Crispin Ct. ME17: Cox 2F 49
Crispin Rd. ME2: Strood 7G 9
Crispin Way ME19: Kings H 1B 40
Criterion Pas. *ME12: S'ness 1A 52*
(off High St.)
Crittenden Cotts.
ME15: E Far 1C 48
Crocus Av. ME12: Minst 7J 53
Crocus Dr. ME10: Rod, Sit 6D 28
Croft, The ME19: Leyb 1F 35
Croft Av. ME10: Sit 3G 29
Croft Cl. ME5: Lord W 1G 33
Crofters, The ME8: Rain 2F 23
Croindene Ct. ME12: Minst 6G 53
Cromer Rd. ME2: Strood 7K 9
Cromers Rd. ME10: Sit 7C 28
Crompton Gdns.
ME15: Maid 5K 7 (1A 44)
Cromwell Rd. ME12: S'ness 4A 52
ME14: Maid 2K 7 (6K 37)
Cromwell Ter.
ME4: Chat'm 6D 4 (5E 14)
Cronin Cl. ME20: Lark 6B 30
Crosier Ct. ME9: Upc 5K 17
Crosley Rd. ME7: Gill 5H 15
Crossfield Wlk. ME6: Snod 7C 18
Cross Keys ME14: Bear 7H 39
Cross Keys Cotts. ME14: Bear 7J 39
Cross La. *ME10: Sit 1C 28*
(off Oyster Cl.)
Cross St. ME2: Strood 7K 9
ME4: Chat'm 4D 4 (4E 14)
ME7: Gill 3G 5 (2G 15)
ME12: S'ness 2B 52
ME14: Maid 5K 37
Cross Way ME1: Roch 5K 13
Crossway ME5: Chat'm 3C 20
Crossways ME10: Sit 6C 28
ME17: Cha S 4G 51
Crow Cnr. ME1: Roch 5C 6
Crow La. ME1: Roch 6C 6 (3A 14)
Crownfields ME14: Weav 7E 38
Crown Grn. DA12: Shorne 4A 8
Crown Ho. ME1: Roch 7A 6
Crown La. DA12: Shorne 4A 8
Crown Quay La. ME10: Sit 3D 28
Crown Rd. ME10: Sit 2C 28
Crown St. ME7: Gill 3J 5 (2H 15)
Crown Wharf
ME2: Med E 2E 6 (1B 14)
Crown Wood Ct. *ME15: Maid 6D 44*
(off Wallis Av.)
Crowton Ct. *ME6: Snod 2D 30*
(off May St.)
Croydon Cl. ME5: Lord W 5G 21
Crundale ME14: Maid 2K 7 (6K 37)
Crundale Rd. ME8: Gill 5C 16
Crusader Cl. ME8: Gill 1B 22
Crutches La. ME2: Strood 6D 8
ME3: High'm, Strood 6D 8
Cryalls La. ME10: Sit 6K 25
Cucknolds Cnr. ME3: High'm 1E 8
Cuckoowood Av.
ME14: Maid 3J 37
Cudham Cl. ME14: Maid 5B 38
Culpeper Cl.
ME2: Med E 3E 6 (2B 14)
ME17: Holl 2F 47
Culpepper Rd. ME8: Parkw 5D 22
ME17: Cox 2E 48
Cumberland Av. ME15: Maid 4C 44
Cumberland Rd. ME4: Chat'm 1F 15
ME7: Gill 1G 5 (1G 15)
Cunningham Cres.
ME5: Chat'm 1E 20
Cunningham Ho.
ME1: Roch 7A 6 (4K 13)
Curlew Cres. ME2: Strood 2E 12
(not continuous)
Curtis Way ME1: Roch 2B 20
Curves
Senacre Wood 5E 44
Curzon Rd.
ME4: Chat'm 7C 4 (5D 14)
ME14: Maid 5K 37
Cut, The ME4: Chat'm 1C 4 (2D 14)
Cutbush & Corrall Ct.
ME14: Maid 7A 38

60 A-Z Maidstone & Medway Towns

Edwards Cl.—Forstal Cotts.

Edwards Cl. ME6: Snod 7C 18
ME8: Wigm 4C 22
Edward St. ME2: Strood 1K 13
ME4: Chat'm 7E 4 (5E 14)
ME12: S'ness 1A 52
(off Charles St.)
Edward Wlk. ME19: E Mal 3G 35
Edwina Av. ME12: Minst 5G 53
Edwin Pl. ME8: Gill 2C 22
Edwin Rd. ME8: Gill 1B 22
Edyngham Cl. ME10: Kems'y 6E 26
Egerton Rd. ME14: Maid 4H 37
Eglington Dr. ME3: Wain 4B 10
Egremont Rd. ME15: Bear 2E 44
Egret Cl. ME4: St Mary 5F 11
Egypt Pl. ME14: Bear 7H 39
Eight Dock E. Rd.
ME4: Chat'm 6E 10
Elaine Av. ME2: Strood 1G 13
Elaine Ct. ME2: Strood 2G 13
Elan Cl. ME19: Kings H 7E 34
Elder Ct. ME8: Wigm 3B 22
Elder Wlk. ME12: Minst 7H 53
Eldon St. ME4: Chat'm . . .4D 4 (4E 14)
Eleanor Ct. ME8: Wigm 6C 22
Eleanor Dr. ME10: Sit 6D 26
Elgin Gdns. ME2: Strood 3F 13
Elham Cl. ME8: Gill 6B 16
Eling Ct. ME15: Maid 4K 43
Elizabeth Ct. ME5: Chat'm 2E 20
ME8: Gill 7C 16
Elizabeth Fry Ter.
ME1: Roch 1K 13
Elizabeth Ho. ME1: Roch 7C 6
ME14: Maid 1J 7 (5K 37)
Elizabeth Smith Ct.
ME19: E Mal 4G 35
Ellenswood Cl. ME15: Bear 3E 44
Ellingham Leas ME15: Maid 5B 44
Elliotts Way ME5: Chat'm 3B 20
Ellison Way ME8: Rain 6G 17
Elm Av. ME2: C'den, Upnor 3E 10
ME3: C'den 3E 10
ME4: Chat'm 7C 14
Elm Cl. ME3: High'm 4E 8
Elm Ct. Village ME7: Gill 6J 21
Elm Cres. ME19: E Mal 3G 35
Elmfield ME8: Gill 5A 16
Elmfield Ct. ME17: Cox 2F 49
Elm Gro. ME10: Sit 3F 29
ME15: Maid 1A 44
Elmhurst Gdns. ME4: Chat'm 5B 14
Elm La. ME12: Minst 7J 53
Elmley Marshes Nature Reserve
. . . . .2J 27
Elm Rd. ME3: Hoo W 4J 11
ME7: Gill 2J 15
Elmscroft Farm Cotts.
ME15: W Far 6B 42
Elmstone Cl. ME16: Maid 2E 42
Elmstone La. ME16: Maid 2E 42
Elmstone Rd. ME8: Gill 2D 22
Elm Tree Av. ME9: Iwade 2B 26
Elmtree Dr. ME1: Roch 6J 13
Elm Vs. ME3: C'den 2D 10
Elm Wlk. ME20: Aylfd 2B 36
Elmwood Rd. ME3: C'den 1D 10
Elphinstone Ho. ME14: Maid 4J 37
Elstar Pl. ME19: Kings H 1C 40
Elvington Cl. ME16: Maid 6G 37
Ely Cl. ME8: Rain 6E 16
Ely Ho. ME15: Maid 5C 44
Embassy Cl. ME7: Gill 7K 15
Emerald Cl. ME1: Roch 2B 20
Emerald Cres. ME10: Sit 1A 28
Emerald Wlk. ME19: Kings H . . .7E 34
Emily Rd. ME5: W'slade 3F 21
Emmeline Cl. ME8: Rain 6D 16
Empire Rd. ME2: Strood 3G 13
Empress Ho. ME2: Strood 1A 6
Emsworth Gro. ME14: Maid 5C 38
Endeavour Foyer, The
ME4: Chat'm 6F 15
(off Shipwrights Av.)
Englefield Cres. ME3: Cli W 2A 10
Ennerdale Ho. *ME15: Maid 5D 44*
(off Westmorland Grn.)
Enterprise Bus. Est.
ME2: Med E 1C 14
Enterprise Centre, The
ME5: Lord W 2G 33
Enterprise Cl. ME2: Med E 7B 10
Enterprise Rd. ME15: Maid 3K 43
Epaul La. ME1: Roch 4B 6 (2A 14)
Epps Ct. *ME2: Strood 7K 9*
(off Goddington Rd.)
Epps Rd. ME10: Sit 4C 28
Epsom Cl. ME15: Maid 6E 44
ME19: W Mal 3B 34
Erith Cl. ME14: Pen H 3K 37
Ernest Dr. ME16: Alltn 6E 36
Ernest Rd.
ME4: Chat'm 7D 4 (5E 14)
Eslington Ct. *ME2: Strood 6K 9*
(off Bill St. Rd.)
Esmonde Ho. *ME7: Gill 2E 14*
(off Flaxmans Ct.)
Esplanade ME1: Roch 7A 6 (5J 13)
ME2: Strood 3A 6 (2K 13)
ME12: S'ness 1B 52
Esplanade, The *ME12: S'ness . . .2C 52*
(off Royal Rd.)
Essex Rd. ME2: Hall'g 4C 18
ME15: Maid 6D 44
Estelle Cl. ME1: Roch 2B 20
Esther Ct. ME10: Sit 6C 26
Estuary Reach *ME7: Gill 2E 14*
(off Pleasant Row)
Estuary Rd. ME12: S'ness 3B 52
Ethelbert Rd.
ME1: Roch 7B 6 (4A 14)
Ethel Maud Ct.
ME7: Gill 1J 5 (1H 15)
Eton Cl. ME5: W'slade 5D 20
Eurolink Bus. Pk. ME10: Sit 1F 29
Eurolink Commercial Pk.
ME10: Sit 2E 28
Eurolink Ind. Cen. ME10: Sit 2G 29
Eurolink Ind. Est. ME10: Sit 3F 29
Eurolink Way ME10: Sit 3D 28
Eustace Cres. ME2: Strood 4G 13
Eva Rd. ME7: Gill 5H 15
Eveas Dr. ME10: Sit 3G 29
Evelyn Cl. ME2: Strood . . .1B 6 (7A 10)
Evelyn Ho. ME2: Strood 7A 10
Evelyn Rd. ME16: Maid 1H 43
Everest Dr. ME3: Hoo W 3J 11
Everest La. ME2: Strood 6K 9
Everest M. ME3: Hoo W 3J 11
Everglades, The ME7: Hpstd 3K 21
Evergreen Cl. ME3: High'm 4D 8
ME7: Hpstd 4A 22
ME9: Iwade 2B 26
ME19: Leyb 1F 35
Eversley Cl. ME16: Alltn 4F 37
Ewart Rd. ME4: Chat'm 7C 14
Ewell Av. ME19: W Mal 3B 34
Ewell La. ME15: W Far 6K 41
Exchange Ct. *ME10: Sit 4E 28*
(off Gaze Hill Av.)
Exchange Studio ***3J 7***
(within Hazlitt Arts Cen.)
Exeter Ho. ME15: Maid 5C 44
Exeter Wlk. ME1: Roch 2A 20
Exmouth Rd. ME7: Gill . . .1H 5 (1G 15)
Exton Cl. ME5: Lord W 7G 21
Exton Gdns. ME14: Weav 6E 38
Eye, The ME4: Chat'm . . .3C 4 (3D 14)
EYHORNE GREEN **2D 46**
EYHORNE STREET **2D 46**
Eyhorne St. ME17: Holl 3D 46
Eylesden Ct. ME14: Bear 7H 39
Eynsford Rd. ME16: Alltn 4G 37

F

Factory Cotts. ME1: Woul 5E 18
ME2: Cux 5F 13
Fagus Cl. ME5: W'slade 1F 33
Fairbourne La. ME17: H'shm 7K 47
Fairfax Cl. ME8: Parkw 4D 22
Fairfax Ct. ME14: Maid 3J 7
Fairfax Ho. ME15: Maid 7D 44
Fairhurst Dr. ME15: E Far 1E 48
Fairlawn Cl. ME18: Tstn 4H 41
Fairlead Rd. ME1: Roch 7B 14
Fairleas ME10: Sit 5F 29
Fairmeadow
ME14: Maid 1G 7 (7J 37)
(not continuous)
Fairservice Cl. ME10: Sit 2G 29
Fairview Av. ME8: Wigm 4B 22
Fairview Cotts. ME15: Loose 7J 43
ME15: W Far 6B 42
Fairview Dr. ME3: High'm 3D 8
Fairview Rd. ME10: Sit 4E 28
Fairway, The ME1: Roch 7A 14
ME10: Sit 6C 28
Fairway Bus. Pk. ME10: Sit 7H 27
Fairway Cl. ME1: Roch 7A 14
Falcon Ct. ME10: Sit 5E 28
Falcon Gdns. ME12: Minst 5K 53
Falcon Grn. ME20: Lark 2G 35
Falkland Pl. ME5: W'slade 1C 32
Fallowfield ME5: Chat'm 1F 21
ME10: Sit 5E 28
Fallowfield Cl. ME14: Weav 7D 38
Fanconi Rd. ME5: Lord W 6F 21
Fancy Row ME14: Bear 6H 39
Fane Way ME8: Parkw 5C 22
Fans La. ME9: Iwade 2B 26
FANT **1G 43**
Fant La. ME16: Maid 2E 42
Faraday Ho. ME1: Roch 6D 6
Faraday Rd. ME14: Pen H 4B 38
Fareham Wlk. ME15: Maid 6E 44
Farington Cl. ME16: Maid 7E 36
Farleigh Bri. ME16: E Far 4D 42
Farleigh Ct. ME16: Maid 2D 42
FARLEIGH GREEN **6B 42**
Farleigh Hill ME15: Maid 3H 43
Farleigh Hill Retail Pk.
ME15: Maid 3H 43
Farleigh La. ME16: Maid 2D 42
Farleigh Trad. Est.
ME15: Maid 2H 43
Farley Cl. ME5: Lord W 7H 21
Farm Cotts. ME15: Maid 3C 44
Farm Cres. ME10: Sit 5E 28
Farmdale Av. ME1: Roch 6H 13
Farmer Cl. ME17: Leeds 6B 46
Farm Hill Av. ME2: Strood 6H 9
Farm Rd. ME5: W'slade 6C 20
Farnborough Cl. ME16: Maid 2F 43
Farne Cl. ME15: Maid 6K 43
Farnham Cl. ME8: Rain 7H 17
Farningham Cl. ME14: Maid 5B 38
Farraday Cl. ME1: Roch 1B 20
Farrier Cl. ME14: Weav 6D 38
Farriers Ct. ME8: Rain 1J 23
Farrows, The ME15: Maid 5A 44
Farrows Wlk. *ME15: Maid 5A 44*
(off The Farrows)
Fartherwell Av.
ME19: W Mal 3B 34
Fartherwell Rd. ME19: W Mal . . .4A 34
FARTHING CORNER **6E 22**
Farthings Cotts. ME14: S'lng 2J 37
Fathom Ho. ME1: Roch 7A 14
Fauchon's Cl. ME14: Bear 1E 44
Fauchon's La. ME14: Bear 1E 44
Fawley Cl. ME14: Maid 4H 37
Fay Cl. ME1: Roch 5J 13
Featherbed La. ME9: Bob 4C 26
Featherby Rd. ME8: Gill 6A 16
(not continuous)
Featherbys Cotts. ME7: Gill 2K 15
Felderland Cl. ME15: Maid 7C 44
Felderland Dr. ME15: Maid 7D 44
Felderland Rd. ME15: Maid 7D 44
Feldspar Cl. ME5: W'slade 1D 32
ME10: Sit 1B 28
Fellows Cl. ME8: Wigm 3B 22
Fennel Cl. ME1: Roch 5J 13
ME12: Minst 7H 53
ME16: Maid 1E 42
Fernbank Cl. ME5: W'slade 1C 32
Ferndale Cl. ME12: Minst 6D 52
Ferndale Rd. ME7: Gill 4K 5 (3J 15)
Ferndown Cl. ME7: Hpstd 4A 22
Fernhill Rd. ME16: Maid 2D 42
Fernleigh ME10: Sit 5B 28
Fernleigh Ri. ME20: Dit 1J 35
Fernleigh Ter. ME10: Sit 5B 28
Ferns, The ME20: Lark 1J 35
Fern Wlk. ME10: Sit 2G 29
Ferrier Cl. ME8: Parkw 5E 22
Ferry La. ME1: Woul 5E 18
Ferry Rd. ME2: Hall'g 5D 18
ME9: Iwade 2C 26
Ffinch Cl. ME20: Dit 3A 36
Field Cl. ME5: Chat'm 3C 20
Fielder Cl. ME10: Sit 2G 29
Fielding Dr. ME20: Lark 7C 30
Fieldings, The ME10: Sit 5C 28
Fields, The ME3: Hoo W 1H 11
Fields La. ME18: W'bury 5F 41
Field Vw. Cl. ME12: Minst 6C 52
Fieldworks Rd. ME7: Gill 1E 1
Fiji Ter. ME14: Maid 4K 3
Filer Rd. ME12: Minst 5E 5
Finch Ct. ME14: Maid 4H 3
Finches, The ME10: Sit 4D 2
Findlay Cl. ME8: Parkw 3D 2
Findley Ho. ME14: Maid 4J 3
Finglesham Ct. ME15: Maid 4B 4
Fintonagh Dr. ME14: Pen H 4A 3
Finwell Rd. ME8: Rain 6G 1
Fire Opal Way ME10: Sit 1B 2
Firethorn Cl. ME7: Gill 2J 1
Firmin Av. ME17: Bou Mo 7C 4
Firs Cl. ME20: Aylfd 2B 3
Firs La. ME17: Holl 2K 4
First Av. ME4: Chat'm 6G 1
ME7: Gill 6J 1
ME12: S'ness 3C 5
Fir Tree Gro. ME5: Lord W 1H 3
Fisher Rd. ME5: Chat'm 2F 2
Fisher St. ME14: Maid 1J 7 (5K 37
Fitzgilbert Cl. ME7: Gill 3A 1
Fitzwilliam Rd. ME14: Weav 6E 3
Five Bells La.
ME1: Roch 7E 6 (4B 14
Five Ways Ct.
ME4: Chat'm 5E 4 (4E 14
FIVE WENTS **3J 5**
Flack Gdns. ME3: Hoo W 2J 1
Flamingo Cl. ME5: Chat'm 2E 2
Flanders Cl. ME10: Kems'y 5D 2
Flaxman Dr. ME16: Alltn 5F 3
Flaxmans Ct.
ME7: Gill 1D 4 (2E 14
Fleet Av. ME12: S'ness 3B 5
Fleet End ME10: Kems'y 3D 2
Fleet Rd. ME1: Roch 7B 1
Fleetwood Cl. ME12: Minst 6H 5
Fletcher Gdns. ME6: Snod 2B 3
Flint Cl. ME10: Kems'y 6C 2
Flint Grn. ME5: Lord W 6G 21
Flood Hatch ME15: Maid 2G 4
Florence Rd.
ME16: Maid 6F 7 (1H 43
Florence St. ME2: Strood 7K 9
Florin Dr. ME1: Roch 4K 1
Flower Ri. ME14: Maid 5J 3
Flume End ME15: Maid 2G 4
Foley St. ME14: Maid 1K 7 (6K 37
Folkestone Ho. *ME15: Maid 6E 4*
(off Fontwell Cl.
Fonblanque Rd.
ME12: S'ness 2C 52
Fontana *ME5: W'slade 6E 2*
(off Walderslade Rd.
Fontwell Cl. ME15: Maid 6E 44
Foord Almshouses
ME1: Roch 5K 13
Foord St. ME1: Roch 7C 6 (4A 14
Foords Wharf ME16: Alltn 4G 37
Fordcombe Cl. ME15: Maid 5E 44
Fordingbridge Cl.
ME16: Alltn 6E 36
Fordwich Cl. ME16: Alltn 4E 36
Fordwich Dr. ME2: Strood 5J 9
Fordwich Grn. ME8: Gill 5C 16
Foremans Barn Rd.
ME15: Hunt 2C 48
Forestdale Rd. ME5: W'slade 2E 32
Forest Dr. ME5: W'slade 7D 20
Foresters Cl. ME5: W'slade 7D 20
Forest Hill ME15: Maid 3J 43
Forest Way ME19: Kings H 1B 40
Forge Cotts. *ME14: Bear 7H 39*
(off The Green
ME17: Bou Mo 2A 50
Forge La. DA12: Shorne 4A 8
ME3: High'm 5E 8
ME7: B'hst, Gill 7K 21
ME7: Gill 2K 5 (1J 15)
ME14: Boxl 7G 33
ME15: E Far 5E 42
ME17: Bou Mo 7E 50
ME17: Leeds 5K 45
Forge Lodge Bungs.
ME15: Maid 3C 44
Forge Mdw. ME17: H'shm 6K 47
Forge Rd. ME10: Sit 1C 28
Formby Rd. ME2: Hall'g 3C 18
Formby Ter. ME2: Hall'g 3C 18
Forsham La. ME17: Sut V 7J 51
FORSTAL **1F 37**
Forstal Cotts. ME20: Aylfd 1E 36

Forstal La.—Grafton Av.

Forstal La. ME17: Cox 1G **49**
ME17: H'shm, Holl 5G **47**
Forstal Rd. ME14: S'lng 1D **36**
ME20: Aylfd 1D **36**
Forsters ME17: L'ly 1K **51**
Forsyth Cl. ME19: E Mal 2H **35**
Forsyth Ct. ME7: Gill 1G **5** (1G **15**)
Fort, The ME1: Roch 4B **14**
Fort Amherst 2C **4** (3D **14**)
Fort Bridgewood ME1: Roch 2K **19**
Fort Pitt Hill
ME4: Chat'm 5A **4** (4C **14**)
Fort Pitt St.
ME4: Chat'm 6A **4** (5C **14**)
Fort St. ME1: Roch 7D **6** (4B **14**)
Fortune Way ME19: Kings H 1C **40**
Forum, The ME10: Sit 3D **28**
Forward Way ME1: Roch 3A **20**
Foster Clarke Dr.
ME17: Bou Mo 7C **44**
Foster Clark Est. ME15: Maid ...2A **44**
Foster St. ME15: Maid 5J **7** (1K **43**)
Fostington Way
ME5: W'slade 1C **32**
Foulds Cl. ME8: Wigm 4B **22**
Foundry Wharf ME1: Roch 4C **14**
Fountain La. ME16: Maid 2D **42**
Fountain Pas. *ME12: S'ness* *2A* ***52***
(off West La.)
Fountain Rd. ME2: Strood 6G **9**
Fountain St. ME10: Sit 3C **28**
Four Acres ME19: E Mal 6J **35**
Four Elms Hill
ME3: C'den, Wain 4C **10**
Fourth Av. ME7: Gill 4J **15**
Fourth Wall *3J* ***7***
(within Hazlitt Arts Cen.)
FOUR WENTS **3E 50**
Four Wents ME17: L'ly 2K **51**
Fourwents Rd. ME3: Hoo W 1H **11**
Fowey Cl. ME5: Lord W 4G **21**
Fowler Cl. ME8: Wigm 6C **22**
Foxburrow Cl. ME8: Parkw 4D **22**
Foxburrow Wood Local Nature Reserve
...................**4E 22**
Foxden Dr. ME15: Bear 3E **44**
Foxglove Cres.
ME5: W'slade 5C **20**
Foxglove Ri. ME14: Maid 4H **37**
Foxglove Row ME2: Hall'g 4B **18**
Foxgrove ME10: Sit 7C **26**
Fox Hill ME9: Bap 4H **29**
Foxley Rd. ME11: Queen 7A **52**
Fox St. ME7: Gill 3G **5** (2G **15**)
Foxtail Cl. ME4: St Mary 5F **11**
Francis Dr. ME5: W'slade 7E **20**
Francis La. ME15: Maid 7E **44**
ME19: Kings H 1E **40**
Frank Apps Cl. ME9: N'tn 3D **24**
Franklin Dr. ME14: Weav 7C **38**
Franklin Rd. ME7: Gill 4J **5** (3H **15**)
Franklins Cotts. ME15: E Far 7F **43**
Franks Ct. ME8: Gill 6B **16**
Frederick Rd.
ME7: Gill 7G **5** (4G **15**)
Frederick St. ME10: Sit 3C **28**
Freelands Rd. ME6: Snod 2B **30**
Freeman Ct. *ME10: Sit* *3C* ***28***
(off Gibson St.)
Freeman Dr. ME10: Sit 2G **29**
Freeman Gdns. ME4: Chat'm ...6D **14**
Freeman Way ME15: Maid 4D **44**
Freesia Cl. ME7: Gill 2K **15**
Fremlins Rd. ME14: Bear 7H **39**
Fremlin Wlk.
ME14: Maid 3H **7** (7J **37**)
Frensham Cl. ME10: Sit 3F **29**
Frensham Wlk. ME5: W'slade ...7D **20**
Freshland Rd. ME16: Maid 7E **36**
Freshwater Rd. ME5: Chat'm 2F **21**
Friars Av. ME5: W'slade 7D **20**
Friars, The (Aylesford Priory)
...................**1B 36**
Friars Ct. ME14: Maid 3K **7** (7K **37**)
Friars Vw. ME20: Aylfd 1B **36**
Friary Pl. ME2: Strood ...1A **6** (1K **13**)
Friary Pct.
ME2: Strood 1A **6** (1K **13**)
Frigenti Pl. ME14: Maid 6A **38**
FRINDSBURY **6A 10**
Frindsbury Hill ME2: Strood 6A **10**
Frindsbury Rd.
ME2: Strood 1A **6** (7K **9**)
Frinstead Wlk. ME16: Alltn 4F **37**
Frinsted Cl. ME8: Gill 5C **16**
Friston Way ME1: Roch 1B **20**
Frithwood Cl. ME15: Bear 3E **44**
Frittenden Rd. ME2: Wain 5B **10**
Frobisher Cl. ME10: Sit 1C **28**
Frobisher Gdns. ME1: Roch 6A **14**
Frog La. ME19: W Mal 3D **34**
Frost Cres. ME5: Chat'm 2E **20**
Froyle Cl. ME16: Alltn 5F **37**
Fruiterer's Cl. ME9: Rod 7E **28**
Fulbert Dr. ME14: Weav 6E **38**
Fullagers Yd. ME4: Chat'm 4C **4**
Fullers Cl. ME14: Bear 7F **39**
Fulmar Av. ME9: Iwade 2C **26**
Fulmar Rd. ME2: Strood 2F **13**
Fulston Mnr. Vista *ME10: Sit* *5D* ***28***
(off Bluebell Dr.)
Fulston Pl. ME10: Sit 4E **28**
Furfield Chase
ME17: Bou Mo 1D **50**
Furfield Cl. ME15: Maid 7D **44**
Furrell's Rd.
ME1: Roch 6D **6** (3B **14**)
Furze Hill Cres. ME12: Minst 7E **52**
Future Ct. ME2: Med E 7C **10**

G

Gable Cotts. ME15: Otham 5G **45**
Gabriel's Hill
ME15: Maid 4J **7** (7K **37**)
Gadby Rd. ME10: Sit 2A **28**
GADSHILL **5E 8**
Gads Hill ME7: Gill 1K **15**
Gagetown Ter. ME14: Maid 4J **37**
Gainsborough Cl. ME8: Gill 3D **22**
ME10: Sit 4K **25**
Gainsborough Dr. ME16: Maid ...7E **36**
Gainsborough Ho. ME1: Roch 6D **6**
Gala Bingo
Chatham ....**5D 4 (4E 14)**
Maidstone ....**4J 7 (7K 37)**
Rochester **4G 13**
Galahad Av. ME2: Strood 2G **13**
Galapagos Ho. ME15: Maid 6C **44**
Galena Cl. ME5: W'slade 1E **32**
ME10: Sit 1A **28**
Gallants La. ME15: E Far 5C **42**
Galleon Cl. ME1: Roch 1A **20**
Galleon Way ME2: Upnor 4D **10**
Galway Rd. ME12: S'ness 2C **52**
Gambit Way ME3: Wain 4B **10**
Gamelan Cres. ME3: Hoo W 1J **11**
Gamelan Wlk. ME3: Hoo W 1J **11**
Gandy's La. ME17: Bou Mo 3B **50**
Garden Cl. ME15: Maid 5D **44**
Garden Ct. ME1: Woul 4E **18**
Gardenia Cl. ME2: Strood 5K **9**
Garden of England Crematorium
ME9: Bob 5A **26**
Garden of England Pk.
ME17: H'shm 5J **47**
Gardens, The ME17: Cox 2F **49**
(not continuous)
Garden St. ME7: Gill 1D **4** (2E **14**)
Garden Wlk. ME15: Maid 1D **44**
Garden Way ME19: Kings H 2B **40**
Gardiner St.
ME7: Gill 3H **5** (2G **15**)
Garfield Rd. ME7: Gill 2J **5** (2H **15**)
Garner Dr. ME19: E Mal 2H **35**
Garrington Cl. ME14: Maid 5B **38**
Garrison Rd. ME12: S'ness 1A **52**
Gascoyne Cl. ME15: Bear 2G **45**
Gas Ho. Rd.
ME1: Roch 4C **6** (2A **14**)
Gas Rd. ME10: Sit 1F **29**
(Eurolink Bus. Pk.)
ME10: Sit 2D **28**
(Mill Way)
Gassons Rd. ME6: Snod 2A **30**
Gatcombe Cl. ME5: W'slade 4E **20**
ME16: Alltn 6F **37**
Gatehouse Lodge
ME15: Maid 2D **44**
Gatekeeper Chase ME8: Rain ...1F **23**
Gatland La. ME16: Maid 3D **42**
Gault Cl. ME15: Bear 2F **45**
Gayhurst Cl. ME8: Gill 3D **22**
Gayhurst Dr. ME10: Sit 2A **28**
Gaze Hill Av. ME10: Sit 4E **28**
Gean Cl. ME5: W'slade 1E **32**
Gemstone Ct. ME10: Sit 1A **28**
Genesta Cl. ME10: Sit 7C **26**
Geneva Av. ME8: Gill 6A **16**
Gentian Cl. ME5: W'slade 5C **20**
(not continuous)
ME14: Weav 6D **38**
George La. ME1: Roch ...4C **6** (2A **14**)
ME17: Leeds 5B **46**
George Marsham Ho.
ME15: Loose 2J **49**
George Parris Ct.
ME12: Minst 6J **53**
George St. ME10: Sit 4F **29**
ME15: Hunt 6D **48**
ME15: Maid 6J **7** (1K **43**)
George Summers Cl.
ME2: Med E 7C **10**
George Wlk. *ME10: Kems'y* *5E* ***26***
(off Reams Way)
Georgian Dr. ME17: Cox 2G **49**
Georgian Way ME8: Wigm 5C **22**
Gerald Av. ME4: Chat'm 6D **14**
Gerrard Av. ME1: Roch 1B **20**
Gerrards Dr. ME10: Sit 5D **28**
Gibbons Rd. ME10: Sit 4K **25**
Gibbs Hill ME18: Nett 7C **40**
Gibraltar Av. ME7: Gill 1E **14**
Gibraltar Hill
ME4: Chat'm 5B **4** (4D **14**)
Gibraltar La. ME14: Maid 3H **37**
Gibson Dr. ME19: Kings H 7A **34**
Gibson St. ME10: Sit 3C **28**
Gidds Pond Cotts.
ME14: Weav 5D **38**
Giddyhorn La.
ME16: Alltn, Maid 7F **37**
(not continuous)
Gifford Cl. ME8: Gill 4C **16**
Gighill Rd. ME20: Lark 7B **30**
Gilbert Cl. ME7: Hpstd 4A **22**
Gilbert Ter. ME14: Maid 4J **37**
Giles Young Ct. *ME10: Sit* *2C* ***28***
(off High St.)
Gill Av. ME2: Wain 4B **10**
Gilletts La. ME19: E Mal 5H **35**
GILLINGHAM ....**4H 5 (3G 15)**
Gillingham Bus. Cen.
ME8: Gill 7K **15**
Gillingham Bus. Pk. ME8: Gill ...7A **16**
Gillingham FC **3J 15**
Gillingham Ga. ME7: Gill 7H **11**
Gillingham Ga. Rd.
ME4: Chat'm 7G **11**
Gillingham Golf Course **6K 15**
Gillingham Grn. ME7: Gill 2J **15**
Gillingham Northern Link Rd.
ME7: Gill 2A **16**
Gillingham Rd.
ME7: Gill 6H **5** (4G **15**)
Gillingham Station (Rail)
...............**4J 5 (3H 15)**
Gill's Cotts. ME1: Roch 4C **14**
Gills Ct. ME2: Med E 7C **10**
Ginsbury Cl. ME2: Med E 2C **14**
Ginsbury Ho. ME2: Med E 2B **14**
Glade, The ME5: W'slade 7E **20**
Gladepoint ME5: Lord W 2G **33**
Gladstone Dr. ME10: Sit 4G **29**
Gladstone Rd.
ME4: Chat'm 7A **4** (6C **14**)
ME14: Pen H 5K **37**
Gladwyn Cl. ME8: Parkw 5D **22**
(not continuous)
Glamford Rd. ME2: Strood 3F **13**
Glamis Cl. ME5: W'slade 4E **20**
Glanville Rd. ME2: Strood 1J **13**
ME7: Gill 5K **5** (3H **15**)
Glasgow Ho. *ME15: Maid* *5D* ***44***
(off Lancashire Rd.)
Glayton Gdns. ME5: W'slade 5D **20**
Gleaming Wood Dr.
ME5: Lord W 2G **33**
Gleaners Cl. ME14: Weav 7D **38**
Gleanings M.
ME1: Roch 6B **6** (3A **14**)
Glebe, The ME2: Cux 6E **12**
Glebe La. ME10: Sit 5F **29**
ME16: Maid 3C **42**
Glebe Mdw. ME18: W'bury 5F **41**
Glebe Rd. ME7: Gill 5J **15**
Glen, The ME12: Minst 4H **53**
(not continuous)
Glenbrook Gro. ME10: Sit 7C **26**
Glencoe Rd.
ME4: Chat'm 7C **4** (6E **14**)
Glendale Rd. ME12: Minst 5H **53**
Gleneagles Ct. ME5: W'slade ...7D **20**
Gleneagles Dr. ME15: Maid 3J **43**
Glenleigh Rd. ME18: W'bury 6E **40**
Glenmore Centre, The
ME10: Sit 1G **29**
Glenton Av. ME19: Kings H 7D **34**
Glenwood Cl. ME5: Chat'm 7G **15**
ME7: Hpstd 3A **22**
ME16: Alltn 6F **37**
Glenwood Dr. ME12: Minst 5H **53**
Glimmer Way ME3: Wain 4B **10**
Glistening Glade ME8: Rain 3E **22**
Globe La. ME4: Chat'm ...3B **4** (3D **14**)
Gloucester Cl. ME8: Rain 1G **23**
Gloucester Rd. ME15: Maid 4C **44**
Glover Cl. ME10: Kems'y 5D **26**
Glovers Cres. ME10: Sit 4D **28**
Glovers Mill ME1: Roch 5B **14**
Glynne Cl. ME8: Gill 3D **22**
Goad Av. ME5: Lord W 6F **21**
Go Ape
Maidstone **6D 46**
Goddard's Castle (remains of)
....................**2J 39**
Godden Rd. ME6: Snod 2B **30**
Godden Way ME8: Gill 4A **16**
Goddings Dr. ME1: Roch 5J **13**
Goddington La. ME17: H'shm ...6J **47**
Goddington Rd. ME2: Strood 7K **9**
Godfrey Cl. ME2: Strood 6H **9**
Godlands, The ME15: Maid 3J **43**
Godwin Cl. ME10: Kems'y 5D **26**
Goldcrest Dr. ME4: St Mary 5G **11**
Gold Dr. ME3: Wain 4B **10**
Golden Ct. ME10: Sit 2F **29**
Golden Wood Cl.
ME5: Lord W 2H **33**
Goldfinch Cl. ME20: Lark 1H **35**
Golding Cl. ME1: Roch 7C **14**
ME20: Dit 2K **35**
Goldings, The ME8: Gill 1C **22**
Goldings Cl. ME19: Kings H 2B **40**
Goldsmith Rd. ME8: Parkw 4E **22**
Gold Star Cen. ME2: Med E 2C **14**
Goldstone Wlk.
ME5: W'slade 1E **32**
Goldsworth Dr. ME2: Strood 6J **9**
Goldthorne Cl. ME14: Maid 6B **38**
Gooch Cl. ME16: Alltn 3G **37**
Goodall Cl. ME8: Parkw 4E **22**
Goodnestone Rd. ME10: Sit 3F **29**
Goodwin Dr. ME14: Pen H 3A **38**
Goodwin Rd. ME3: Cli W 2A **10**
Goodwood Cl. ME15: Maid 6E **44**
Goose Cl. ME5: Chat'm 2E **20**
Gordon Av. ME11: Queen 7A **52**
Gordon Cl. ME10: Sit 3G **29**
Gordon Ct. ME15: Loose 2H **49**
Gordon Rd. ME2: Strood 7J **9**
ME3: Hoo W 2H **11**
ME4: Chat'm 6E **14**
(Glencoe Rd.)
ME4: Chat'm 1E **14**
(North Rd.)
ME7: Gill 5K **5** (3J **15**)
Gordon Ter. ME1: Roch ...7B **6** (4A **14**)
Gore Ct. Rd. ME10: Sit 5C **28**
ME15: Maid 7E **44**
GORE GREEN **1F 9**
Gore Grn. Rd. ME3: High'm 1F **9**
Gorham Cl. ME6: Snod 3B **30**
Gorham Dr. ME15: Bear 3F **45**
Goring Pl. *ME14: Maid* *3J* ***7***
(off Church St.)
Gorse Av. ME5: W'slade 5C **20**
Gorse Cres. ME20: Dit 3A **36**
Gorse Rd. ME2: Strood 7H **9**
ME10: Sit 2F **29**
Gorst St. ME7: Gill 5H **5** (3G **15**)
Goudhurst Cl.
ME16: Maid 3F **7** (7H **37**)
Goudhurst Ho. *ME15: Maid* *7H* ***7***
(off Coombe Rd.)
Goudhurst Rd. ME8: Gill 5B **16**
Gould Rd. ME5: Lord W 6F **21**
Goulston ME15: W Far 6B **42**
Grace Av. ME16: Alltn 5G **37**
Grace Rd. ME12: S'ness 3A **52**
Grafton Av. ME1: Roch 1C **20**

Grafton Rd. ME10: Sit 3D 28
Grafton Way ME10: Sit 3E 28
Graham Clarke Gallery 3H 7
Graham Cl. ME7: Gill 2D 14
Grainey Fld. ME9: H'lip 5A 24
Grain Rd. ME8: Wigm 5B 22
Grampian Way ME15: Bear 3F 45
Granada St.
ME15: Maid 4J 7 (7K 37)
Granary Cl. ME8: Rain 7F 17
ME14: Weav 6D 38
Grand Ct. ME7: Gill 3G 5
Grandsire Gdns.
ME3: Hoo W 1J 11
GRANGE **2B 16**
Grange, The ME19: E Mal 4H 35
Grange Cl. ME19: Leyb 1D 34
Grange Cotts. ME15: Otham 6H 45
Grange Hill ME5: Chat'm 5F 15
Grange Ho. ME16: Maid 2D 42
Grange La. ME14: Boxl, S'lng . . .1J 37
Grange Rd.
ME2: Strood 1A **6** (1K 13)
ME7: Gill 2J 15
(not continuous)
Grange Rdbt. ME7: Gill 2B 16
Grange Way ME1: Roch 5A 14
Grant Cl. ME8: Gill 7B 16
Grant Dr. ME15: Maid 6C 44
Grant Rd. ME3: Wain 4A 10
Granville Ct. ME14: Maid 5K 37
Granville Pl. ME12: S'ness 2C 52
Granville Rd. ME7: Gill 3J 15
ME12: S'ness 2B 52
ME14: Maid 5K 37
Grapple Rd. ME14: Maid 4J 37
Grasmere Gro. ME2: Strood 5A 10
Grasslands ME17: L'ly 1K 51
Grassmere ME19: Leyb 1G 35
Grassy Glade ME7: Hpstd 3B 22
Gravelly Bottom Rd.
ME17: Kgswd 2K 51
Gravel Wlk.
ME1: Roch 6C **6** (3B 14)
Graveney Cl. ME3: Cli W 2B 10
Graveney Rd. ME15: Maid 5E 44
Gravesend Rd. DA12: Shorne 3A 8
ME2: High'm, Strood 5F 9
ME3: High'm 5F 9
Grayling Ct. ME10: Sit 5A 28
Grayling Rd. ME9: Iwade 3B 26
Graylings, The ME1: Roch 5K 13
Grayshott Cl. ME10: Sit 4D 28
Gt. Basin Rd. ME12: S'ness 2A 52
GREAT BUCKLAND **5G 37**
Gt. Easthall Way ME10: Sit 2H 29
(not continuous)
Gt. Ivy Mill Cotts. ME15: Maid . . .5J 43
GREAT LINES **4F 15**
Great Lines ME7: Gill 2E **4** (3E 14)
Great Sth. Av. ME4: Chat'm 7E 14
Grebe Apartments
ME15: Maid 7D 44
(off Wallis Av.)
Grebe Ct. ME20: Lark 2G 35
Grecian St.
ME14: Maid 1K **7** (5K 37)
Green, The ME12: Minst 3H 53
ME14: Bear 7H 39
ME15: E Far 5E 42
ME15: W Far 7B 42
ME17: Bou Mo 2A 50
ME19: W Mal 3D 34
Greenacre Cl. ME5: W'slade 4E 20
Greenbank ME5: Chat'm 1F 21
Greenbank Cl. ME7: Hpstd 4A 22
Greenborough Cl.
ME15: Maid 6D 44
Green Cl. ME1: Roch 6B 14
Green Farm La.
DA12: Shorne 1A 8
Greenfield Cl. ME20: Eccl 4J 31
Greenfield Cotts.
ME14: Boxl 7G 33
Greenfield Rd.
ME7: Gill 3K **5** (2J 15)
Greenfields ME15: Maid 4D 44
Greenfields Cl. ME3: Wain 4B 10
Greenfields Vw. ME15: Maid 4C 44
Greenfinches ME7: Hpstd 3K 21
GREEN HILL **4G 45**
Green Hill
ME15: Otham, Bear 4G 45
Greenhill Cotts.
ME15: Otham 4G 45
Greenhithe ME15: Maid . . .6J **7** (1J 43)
Green La. DA12: Shorne 5A 8
ME9: Rod 7F 29
ME9: S'bry 7A 24
ME17: Bou Mo 2A 50
ME17: L'ly 2K 51
Green La. Cotts. ME17: L'ly 2K 51
Greenlees Cl. ME10: Sit 4K 25
Grn. Porch Cl. ME10: Sit 7D 26
Greensands ME5: W'slade 2G 33
Greensands Rd. ME15: Bear 2F 45
Green's Cotts. ME15: E Far 1D 48
Greenshanks ME9: Iwade 3C 26
Greenside ME15: Maid 1A 44
Greensleeves Way
ME19: Kings H 1D 40
Green St. ME7: Gill 4G **5** (3G 15)
Greenvale Gdns. ME8: Gill 6B 16
Greenview Wlk. ME7: Gill 4A 16
Green Way ME16: Maid 1E 42
Greenway ME5: Chat'm 3B 20
Greenway Ct. Rd.
ME17: Holl 2F 47
GREENWAY FORSTAL **5H 47**
Greenways ME10: Sit 4F 29
ME14: Weav 6E 38
Greenwich Cl. ME5: Lord W 5F 21
ME16: Maid 7G 37
Gregory Cl. ME8: Parkw 5E 22
ME10: Kems'y 6E 26
Grenadier Cl. ME8: Rain 6H 17
ME15: Bear 2E 44
Gresham Cl. ME8: Rain 7F 17
Gresham Rd. ME17: Cox 2G 49
Greyfriars Cl. ME16: Maid 6G 37
Greystones Rd. ME15: Bear 2F 45
Grey Wethers ME14: S'lng 6C 32
Grieveson Ho. ME4: Chat'm 4D 4
Griffin Ct. ME7: Gill 2K 15
Grizedale Cl. ME1: Roch 1B 20
Groombridge Dr. ME7: Gill 2K 15
Groombridge Sq.
ME15: Maid 6E 44
Grooms, The ME2: Hall'g 4C 18
Grosvenor Av.
ME4: Chat'm 7A **4** (5C 14)
Grosvenor Ct. ME16: Maid 1F 43
Grosvenor Ho. *ME15: Maid 7E 44*
(off Wallis Av.)
Grosvenor Rd. ME8: Gill 7K 15
Grove, The ME14: Bear 1F 45
Grove Ct. ME2: Strood 1A 6
GROVE END **7A 28**
GROVE GREEN **6D 38**
Grove Grn. La. ME14: Weav 6D 38
Grove Grn. Rd. ME14: Weav 6E 38
GROVEHURST **5D 26**
Grovehurst Av.
ME10: Kems'y 6D 26
Grovehurst Rd.
ME9: Iwade, Kems'y 3C 26
ME10: Kems'y, Sit 4C 26
Grove La. ME15: Hunt 5A 48
Grove Pk. Av. ME10: Sit 4K 25
Grove Rd. ME2: Hall'g 4A 18
ME2: Strood 1A **6** (7K 9)
ME4: Chat'm 6F 15
ME7: Gill 2A 16
ME15: Maid 6B 44
Groves, The ME6: Snod 3B 30
Grovewood Ct. ME14: Weav 7D 38
Grovewood Dr. Nth.
ME14: Weav 6D 38
Grovewood Dr. Sth.
ME14: Weav 7C 38
Grovewood Halt ME14: Weav 7E 38
Guardian Ct. ME8: Rain 7C 16
Gudgeon Cres. ME3: Hoo W 1J 11
Guelder Rose Dr.
ME3: Hoo W 1J 11
Guildford Gdns. ME2: Strood 2E 12
Guildford Ho. ME15: Maid 5C 44
Guildhall Mus.
Rochester 4B 6
Guinness Dr. ME3: Wain 5K 9
Gullands ME17: L'ly 1K 51
Gundulph Rd. ME1: Roch 4C 14
ME4: Roch 4A **4** (4C 14)
Gundulph Sq.
ME1: Roch 3B **6** (2A 14)
Gun La. ME2: Strood 1A **6** (1J 13)
Gun La. Bus. Est.
ME2: Strood 1J 13
(off Gun La.)
Gunnis Cl. ME8: Parkw 5D 22
Gun Tower M.
ME1: Roch 7A **6** (4K 13)
Guston Rd. ME14: Maid 5B 38
Guys Ct. ME19: Kings H 1B 40

H

Hackney Rd. ME16: Maid 2F 43
Hadleigh Ct. ME7: Hpstd 6A 22
Hadley Gdns. ME17: Holl 2F 47
Hadlow Rd. ME14: Maid 6B 38
Haig Av. ME1: Roch 7B 14
ME4: Chat'm 6E 14
ME7: Gill 4J 15
Haig Vs. ME3: C'den 2E 10
Halden Cl. ME15: Maid 6E 44
HALE **1J 21**
Hale Rd. ME3: Cli W 2B 10
Hales Ct. ME14: Maid 3J 7
Hales Rd. ME10: Sit 6B 28
Haleys Pl. ME1: Burh 2J 31
Halfpenny Cl. ME16: Barm 2D 42
HALFWAY HOUSES **6E 52**
Halfway Rd. ME12: Minst 3D 52
Half Yoke ME16: Maid 4E 42
Halifax Cl. ME5: Lord W 3F 21
Hall Cl. ME10: Sit 1C 28
HALLING **5C 18**
Halling By-Pass ME2: Hall'g 3C 18
Halling Station (Rail) **4C 18**
Hall Rd. ME1: Woul 7E 18
ME5: Lord W 6G 21
ME20: Aylfd 2B 36
Halls Cotts. ME14: Det 2F 39
Hallsfield Rd. ME5: Blue H 6B 20
Hallwood Cl. ME8: Parkw 4D 22
Hallwood Ho. ME5: Lord W 7G 21
Halstead Wlk. ME16: Alltn 4F 37
Halstow Cl. ME15: Maid 6A 44
Hambledon Ct. ME16: Maid 1E 42
Hambrook Rd. ME6: Snod 7B 18
Hambrook Wlk. ME10: Sit 6D 26
Hamelin Rd. ME7: Gill 1K 21
HAM HILL **4C 30**
Hamilton Cl. ME6: Snod 3A 30
Hamilton Ct. *ME1: Roch 4K 13*
(off Fennel Cl.)
ME5: Chat'm 7G 15
Hamilton Cres. ME10: Sit 4A 28
Hamilton Ho. ME15: Maid 7E 44
Hamilton Rd. ME7: Gill . . .1J **5** (1H 15)
Ham La. ME7: Gill 6H 21
Hammond's Sq. ME6: Snod 2C 30
Hamond Hill
ME4: Chat'm 4A **4** (4C 14)
Hampden Way ME19: Kings H . . .1A 40
Hampshire Cl. ME5: Chat'm 2G 21
Hampshire Dr. ME15: Maid 4B 44
Hampshires, The
ME17: H'shm 6K 47
Hampson Way ME14: Bear 7F 39
Hampton Cl. ME5: W'slade 4E 20
Hampton Rd. ME14: Maid 5B 38
Ham River Hill ME3: Cli W 1J 9
Hamwick Grn. ME5: Lord W 1G 33
Hanbury Cl. ME18: W'bury 5F 41
Hancock Cl. ME2: Strood 6K 9
Hanes Dene ME2: Hall'g 4B 18
Hannah Cl.
ME4: Chat'm 7E **4** (5E 14)
Hanover Cl. ME10: Sit 5C 28
Hanover Ct. ME14: Maid 6A 38
Hanover Dr. ME8: Wigm 5C 22
Hanover Grn. ME20: Lark 7A 30
Hanover Ho. ME2: Strood 1A 6
Hanover Rd. ME17: Cox 2F 49
Hanson Dr. ME15: Loose 3J 49
Hanway ME8: Gill 6A 16
Harbledown Ho. ME16: Maid 2E 42
Harbledown Mnr. *ME8: Gill 5B 16*
(off Goudhurst Rd.)
HARBOUR, THE **7K 51**
Harbour, The ME17: Sut V 7K 51
HARBOURLAND **3A 38**
Harbourland Cl. ME14: Boxl 3A 38
Harbourland Cotts.
ME14: Boxl 3B 38
Harcourt Gdns. ME8: Parkw 5E 22
Hardie Cl. ME19: E Mal 2G 35
Hardinge Cl. ME8: Parkw 5D 22
Hards Town
ME4: Chat'm 5E **4** (4E 14)
Hardwick Ho. ME15: Maid 4D 44
Hardy Cl. ME5: W'slade 3F 21
Hardy Lodge *ME1: Roch 5J 13*
(off Fennel Cl.)
Hardy St. ME14: Maid 1J **7** (5K 37)
Harebell Cl. ME5: W'slade 5C 20
ME14: Weav 6D 38
Haredale Cl. ME1: Roch 2B 20
Hare St. ME4: Chat'm 5F 15
ME12: S'ness 2C 52
Hargreaves Rd. ME10: Sit 2H 29
Harkness Ct. ME10: Sit 3F 29
Harlech Cl. ME2: Strood 6H 9
Harlequin Flds. ME1: Roch 5J 13
Harling Cl. ME17: Bou Mo 7C 44
Harman Ct. ME5: Lord W 6E 20
HARMAN'S CORNER **7K 25**
Harmony Cl. ME10: Sit 4B 28
Harold Av. ME7: Gill 4J 15
Harold Rd. ME2: Cux 5E 12
ME10: Sit 3F 29
Harold St. ME11: Queen 7A 52
Harp Farm Rd. ME14: Boxl 3G 33
Harple La. ME14: Det 2E 38
Harps Av. ME12: Minst 6H 53
Harps Wlk. ME12: Minst 6J 53
Harptree Dr. ME5: Chat'm 4C 20
Harrier Dr. ME10: Sit 5E 28
Harriet Dr. ME1: Roch 5J 13
HARRIETSHAM **6K 47**
Harrietsham Station (Rail) **6K 47**
Harris Gdns. ME10: Sit 2G 29
Harris M. ME7: Gill 6K 15
Harris Pl. ME15: Maid 3H 43
Harris Rd. ME12: S'ness 2C 52
Harrow Cotts. ME17: Leeds 1K 51
Harrow Ct. ME5: Lord W 5G 21
Harrower Dr. ME15: Maid 2A 44
Harrow Rd. ME7: Hpstd 3K 21
Harrow Way ME14: Weav 6D 38
Hartington St.
ME4: Chat'm 6D **4** (5E 14)
Hartley Cl. ME15: Maid 6E 44
Hartley M. ME8: Gill 5B 16
HARTLIP **4K 23**
Hartlip Cl. ME12: S'ness 5B 52
Hartlip Hill ME9: H'lip 2A 24
Hartnup St. ME16: Maid 2F 43
Hartpiece Cl. ME8: Rain 6F 17
Hartridge Farm Mobile Home Pk.
ME15: E Far 5D 42
Hart St. ME16: Maid 5G **7** (1J 43)
Hart St. Commercial Cen.
ME16: Maid 6G **7** (1J 43)
Harty Av. ME8: Wigm 6B 22
Harvel Av. ME2: Strood 1H 13
Harvesters Cl. ME8: Rain 3E 22
Harvesters Way ME14: Weav 7C 38
Harvest Ridge ME19: Leyb 1E 34
Harvey Dr. ME10: Sit 5E 28
Harvey Rd. ME8: Gill 1E 22
Harwood Rd. ME8: Rain 7H 17
Hasledon Cotts. ME3: High'm 1E 8
Haslemere Ind. Est.
ME15: Maid 7E 44
Hasted Rd.
ME2: High'm, Strood 7C 8
ME3: Strood, Wain, High'm
. . . . .7C 8
ME9: N'tn 2D 24
Hasteds ME17: Holl 2E 46
HASTE HILL **2K 49**
Haste Hill Cl.
ME17: Bou Mo 2K 49
Haste Hill Rd. ME17: Bou Mo . . .2K 49
Hastings Rd.
ME15: Maid 5K **7** (1A 44)
Hatfield Rd. ME2: Strood 7J 9
Hathaway Ct.
ME1: Roch 5A **6** (3K 13)
ME8: Gill 1D 22
Hatherall Rd. ME14: Maid 5A 38
Hatton Rd. ME5: Lord W 6G 21
Havant Wlk. ME15: Maid 6E 44
Haven Cl. ME1: Roch 6A 14
ME17: Sut V 5K 51
Haven St. ME3: Wain . . . .1K **9** & 3B 10
Haven Way ME4: St Mary 6F 11
Havisham Cl. ME1: Roch 6B 14

Manningham Ho.—Mill La.

Manningham Ho.
ME19: E Mal 5G 35
Manor Cl. ME14: Bear 1G 45
Manor Cotts. ME17: L'ly 7H 45
Manor Ct. ME7: Gill 4C 16
ME14: Bear 1G 45
Manor Fld. DA12: Shorne 4A 8
Manor Flds. ME15: Maid 4C 44
Manor Gdns. ME5: W'slade 6D 20
Manor Gro. ME10: Sit 4B 28
Manor Ho. ME7: Gill 2E 14
Manor Ho. Dr. ME16: Maid 1G 43
Manor La. ME1: Roch 5H 13
ME17: Holl 1F 47
Manor M. ME4: Chat'm . . .4B 4 (4D 14)
Manor Pk. Country Pk. 4C 34
Manor Ri. ME14: Bear 7G 39
Manor Rd.
ME4: Chat'm 4B 4 (4D 14)
Manor St. ME7: Gill 1D 4 (2E 14)
Mansel Dr. ME1: Roch 6J 13
Mansfield Dr. ME9: Iwade 3B 26
Mansfield Pl. *ME15: Maid 6C 44*
(off St Catherine's Rd.)
Mansfield Wlk. ME16: Maid 2H 43
Mansion Cotts. ME15: Maid 1D 44
Mansion Row ME7: Gill . . .1E 4 (2E 14)
Mantle Cl. ME10: Sit 2H 29
Manwood Cl. ME10: Sit 5D 28
Maple Av. ME7: Gill 3J 15
ME16: Alltn 5F 37
Maple Cl. ME20: Lark 1H 35
Maple Rd. ME2: Strood 2H 13
Maples, The ME12: Minst 6H 53
Maplesden Cl. ME16: Barm 1C 42
Maple St. ME12: S'ness 3C 52
Maplins Cl. ME8: Rain 7F 17
Mara Ct. ME4: Chat'm 7D 14
Marathon Paddock
ME7: Gill 6K 5 (4H 15)
Marble Cl. ME7: Gill 2K 15
Marc Brunel Way
ME4: Chat'm 1E 14
Marconi Way ME1: Roch 2B 20
Mardale Cl. ME8: Rain 7G 17
Marden Ho. *ME15: Maid 2K 43*
(off Coombe Rd.)
Marden Rd. ME2: Strood 6A 10
Mardhuran Ct. ME2: Strood 1J 13
Mareda Ct. ME19: Kings H 7D 34
Margate Cl. ME7: Gill 2J 15
Margetts La. ME1: Burh 1F 31
Margetts Pl. ME2: Upnor 4E 10
Marian Av. ME12: Minst 5G 53
Marigold Dr. ME10: Sit 6D 28
Marigold Way ME16: Maid 1D 42
Marina Dr. ME12: Minst 5G 53
Marina Hgts. ME7: Gill 7H 11
Marina Point E. ME4: Chat'm . . .6E 10
Marina Point W.
ME4: Chat'm 6E 10
Marine Dr. ME3: Hoo W 4J 11
Marine Pde.
ME12: Minst, S'ness 2D 52
Mariners, The
ME1: Roch 7A 6 (4K 13)
Mariners Vw. ME7: Gill 1K 15
MARINE TOWN 3C 52
Marine Vw. ME4: St Mary 6F 11
Marion Cl. ME5: W'slade 7E 20
Marion Cres. ME15: Maid 3A 44
Maritime Bus. Cen.
ME2: Med E 7B 10
Maritime Cl. ME2: Med E 7B 10
Maritime Ct. *ME4: Gill 2D 14*
(off Dock Rd.)
Maritime Way
ME4: Chat'm, St Mary 7E 10
Marjoram Dr. ME10: Sit 6D 28
Market Bldgs.
ME14: Maid 3H 7 (7J 37)
Market Pl.
ME4: Chat'm 5E 4 (4E 14)
Markham Cotts.
ME15: W Far 6B 42
Mark St. ME4: Chat'm 7E 4 (6E 14)
Marlborough Pde.
ME16: Barm 2C 42
(off Beverley Rd.)
Marlborough Rd.
ME7: Gill 6F 5 (4F 15)
Marley Rd. ME3: Hoo W 1H 11
Marley Way ME1: Roch 6A 14
Marlow Copse ME5: W'slade 1D 32
Marlowe Rd. ME20: Lark 7B 30
MARLPIT 3D 50
Marquis Dr. ME7: Hpstd 6B 22
Marr Cl. ME12: Minst 5F 53
Marshall Rd. ME8: Gill 2C 22
Marsham Cres. ME17: Cha S . . .4G 51
Marsham St.
ME14: Maid 3K 7 (7K 37)
Marsham Way ME2: Hall'g 4C 18
Marsh Ri. ME10: Kems'y 5E 26
Marsh Rd. ME2: Hall'g 4C 18
Marsh St. ME2: Strood . . .1A 6 (1K 13)
Marsh Vw. ME12: Minst 3G 53
Marsh Way ME20: Lark 6C 30
Marstan Cl. ME9: Upc 6K 17
Marston Cl. ME5: W'slade 6C 20
Marston Dr. ME14: Maid 6A 38
Marston Wlk. ME5: W'slade 6C 20
Martin Ct. ME7: Hpstd 6B 22
ME10: Kems'y 4D 26
Martin Rd. ME2: Strood 7K 9
Martins Cl. ME3: High'm 1F 9
Martin Sq. ME20: Lark 1H 35
(not continuous)
Mary Ct. ME4: Chat'm 7E 4 (6E 14)
Mary Dukes Pl.
ME15: Maid 5K 7 (1A 44)
Maryland Ct. ME8: Parkw 4E 22
Maryland Dr. ME16: Barm 2C 42
Mary Last Cl. ME6: Snod 3A 30
Masefield Dr. ME3: Cli W 1A 10
Masefield Rd. ME20: Lark 6B 30
Mason Way ME3: Wain 5K 9
Massey Cl. ME15: Maid 3K 43
Matfield Cres. ME14: Maid 6B 38
Matilda Cl. ME8: Gill 7B 16
Matterdale Gdns.
ME16: Barm 2B 42
Matthews Ct. ME7: Gill . . .5J 5 (3H 15)
Matts Hill Rd. ME9: H'lip 7D 22
Maunders Cl. ME5: Chat'm 1G 21
Mauritius Ho. *ME15: Maid 6D 44*
(off St Catherine's Rd.)
Maximilian Dr. ME2: Hall'g 5D 18
Maxton Cl. ME14: Weav 6E 38
Maxwell Dr. ME16: Alltn 5E 36
Maxwell Rd. ME7: Gill . . .2D 4 (3E 14)
Mayfair ME2: Strood 6A 10
Mayfair Av. ME15: Maid 4K 43
Mayfield Cl. ME5: W'slade 1E 32
ME8: Rain 6E 16
Mayfield Cotts.
ME14: Bear 7H 39
Mayflower Ho. ME1: Roch 7A 6
Mayford Rd. ME5: Lord W 7H 21
Maylam Gdns. ME10: Sit 5K 25
Maynard Pl. ME5: Chat'm 6H 15
Maypole Dr. ME19: Kings H 1D 40
May Rd. ME1: Roch 5A 14
ME7: Gill 6F 5 (4F 15)
Mays Cotts. ME15: E Far 1D 48
(Green's Cotts.)
ME15: E Far 4B 42
(St Helens La.)
May St. ME2: Cux 6D 12
ME6: Snod 2D 30
May Ter. ME7: Gill 1E 14
Maytum's Cotts. ME17: Lint 5G 49
Mayweed Av. ME5: W'slade 5C 20
Mead, The ME19: Leyb 1F 35
Mead Grn. ME5: Lord W 6G 21
Meadow Bank ME19: W Mal 3D 34
Meadow Bank M.
ME19: W Mal 3D 34
Meadowbank Rd.
ME4: Chat'm 5E 4 (4F 15)
Meadow Brown Vw.
ME9: Iwade 3B 26
Meadow Cl. ME2: Hall'g 5A 18
ME5: W'slade 4D 20
ME9: Iwade 2B 26
Meadow Cres. ME2: Hall'g 5A 18
Meadowdown ME14: Weav 7D 38
Meadowdown Cl. ME7: Hpstd . . .5A 22
Meadow Rise ME9: Iwade 2B 26
Meadows, The ME10: Sit 5D 28
ME15: Maid 2H 43
Meadowsweet Vw.
ME4: St Mary 5F 11
Meadowsweet Wlk.
ME10: Sit 5D 28
(off Bluebell Dr.)
Meadow Vw. ME5: Chat'm 4D 20
ME12: Minst 3G 53
Meadow Vw. Rd.
ME17: Bou Mo 2A 50
Meadow Wlk. ME6: Snod 3B 30
ME15: Maid 1A 44
Meadow Way ME1: Woul 4E 18
Meads Avenue, The
ME10: Sit 7B 26
Meadside Wlk. ME5: Chat'm 3D 20
Mecca Bingo
Sittingbourne 3D 28
Medina Rd. ME20: Dit 2K 35
Medlar Gro. ME7: Hpstd 5A 22
Medlars, The ME14: Maid 5C 38
Medvale Ho. ME15: Maid 5K 7
MEDWAY CITY ESTATE . . .1E 6 (1C 14)
Medway Cl. ME10: Sit 3B 28
Medway Ct. ME20: Aylfd 1C 36
Medway Crematorium
ME5: Blue H 1C 32
Medway Cruising Club 1J 15
Medway Ent. Cen.
ME2: Med E 7B 10
Medway Gdns. ME4: Chat'm 1D 14
Medway Hgts. ME4: Roch 4A 4
Medway Little Theatre
. . . . .6D 6 (3B 14)
MEDWAY MARITIME HOSPITAL
. . . . .7F 5 (4F 15)
Medway Motor Yacht Club 6F 13
Medway Outdoor Education 1J 15
Medway Pk. 2F 5 (2F 15)
Medway Pl. ME1: Woul 5E 18
ME6: Snod 1D 30
Medway Rd. ME7: Gill . . .1G 5 (1G 15)
(not continuous)
ME12: S'ness 3B 52
Medway Sailability Club 4E 10
MEDWAY SERVICE AREA 6F 23
Medway St.
ME4: Chat'm 3B 4 (3D 14)
ME14: Maid 4H 7 (7J 37)
Medway Ter. *ME18: W'bury 6E 40*
(off Maidstone Rd.)
Medway Towns Rowing Club . . .4J 13
Medway Trad. Est.
ME16: Maid 6H 7
Medway Tunnel ME2: Med E 7D 10
ME4: Chat'm 7D 10
Medway Valley Leisure Pk.
ME2: Strood 4G 13
Medway Vs. ME15: E Far 5E 42
Medway Yacht Club 4E 10
Meeres Ct. La. ME10: Sit 2G 29
Meeting Ho. La.
ME4: Chat'm 4C 4 (4D 14)
Megby Cl. ME8: Parkw 3D 22
Melba Cl. ME19: Kings H 7E 34
Melbourne Rd.
ME4: Chat'm 7D 4 (5E 14)
Melford Dr. ME16: Maid 7E 36
Mellor Row ME10: Kems'y 5D 26
Melody Cl. ME8: Wigm 5C 22
Melrose Av. ME19: Kings H 1D 40
Melrose Cl. ME15: Maid 5K 43
Melville Ct.
ME4: Chat'm 1C 4 (2D 14)
Melville Rd.
ME15: Maid 5K 7 (1K 43)
Menin Rd. ME10: Kems'y 5D 26
Menzies Ct. ME12: Minst 7G 53
Mercer Cl. ME20: Lark 6D 30
Mercer Ct. ME5: W'slade 1C 32
Mercers Pl. ME19: Kings H 2B 40
Mercer Way ME17: Cha S 4G 51
Mercian Rd. ME3: Hoo W 2H 11
Mercury Cl. ME1: Roch 6J 13
Meredith Cl. ME17: Leeds 5A 46
MERESBOROUGH 4G 23
Meresborough La.
ME8: Rain 4G 23
ME9: H'lip 4G 23
Meresborough Rd. ME8: Rain . . .6F 23
Mereworth Bus. Cen.
ME18: W'bury 4B 40
Mereworth Cl. ME8: Gill 5A 16
Mereworth Ho. *ME2: Strood 6A 10*
(off Cypress Ct.)
Meridian Ct.
ME16: Maid 3F 7 (7H 37)
Meridian Pk. ME2: Med E 2C 14
Merivale Gro. ME5: W'slade 5E 20
Merleburgh Dr.
ME10: Kems'y 6D 26
Merlin Av. ME20: Lark 1G 35
Merlin Cl. ME10: Sit 4E 28
Merlin Ho. ME4: Chat'm 7F 11
Merlin Way ME7: Gill 5J 5 (3H 15)
Mermaid Cl. ME5: W'slade 3E 20
Merrals Wood Ct.
ME2: Strood 3F 13
(off Wells Rd.)
Merrals Wood Rd.
ME2: Strood 3F 13
Merriams Farm Cotts.
ME17: Leeds 4J 45
Merrick Way ME2: Med E 7C 10
Merrimans Vw. ME5: Chat'm 5G 15
Merry Boys Cotts. ME3: Cliffe . . .1B 10
Merryboys Rd.
ME3: Cliffe, Cli W 1A 10
Merryfields ME2: Strood 6J 9
Merston Ct. ME3: High'm 4E 8
Merton Cl. ME5: Lord W 4G 21
Merton Rd. ME15: Bear 2E 44
Meteor Cl. ME10: Sit 6C 26
Meteor Rd. ME19: Kings H 1A 40
Mews, The ME2: Strood 1H 13
ME10: Sit 5D 28
ME16: Maid 2F 7 (6H 37)
Meyrick Rd. ME12: S'ness 2C 52
Micawber Cl. ME5: W'slade 1E 32
Michele Cotts. ME3: High'm 1E 8
Micketts Gdns. ME10: Sit 5K 25
Middlefields ME8: Rain 1G 23
Middle Mill Rd.
ME19: E Mal 4G 35
Middle Row ME14: Maid 4H 7
Middlesex Rd. ME15: Maid 5C 44
Middle St. ME7: Gill 2E 14
Middleton Cl. ME8: Parkw 5E 22
Middleton Ct. ME10: Sit 3C 28
Middletune Av. ME10: Sit 7C 26
Middleway ME10: Sit 4F 29
Midhurst Ct.
ME15: Maid 5K 7 (1K 43)
Mid Kent Bus. Pk. ME6: Snod . . .3D 30
ME16: Alltn 5E 36
Mid Kent Shop. Centre, The
ME16: Alltn 4F 37
Midley Cl. ME16: Alltn 4F 37
Midsummer Rd. ME6: Snod 2A 30
Mierscourt Cl. ME8: Rain 1G 23
Miers Ct. Rd. ME8: Rain 3E 22
Mierscourt Rd.
ME8: Parkw, Rain 5E 22
Milbourne Gro. ME10: Sit 7C 26
Milburn Rd. ME7: Gill 1H 5 (1G 15)
Miles Pl. ME1: Roch 5B 14
MILE TOWN 2B 52
Mile Town Ind. Pk.
ME12: S'ness 3A 52
Milford Cl. ME16: Maid 6F 37
Military Rd.
ME4: Chat'm 4B 4 (4D 14)
Millbrook ME19: Leyb 2E 34
Millbrook Cl. ME15: Maid 3J 43
Mill Cl. ME2: Strood 6K 9
Mill Ct. ME10: Sit 4E 28
ME15: Maid 4H 7 (7J 37)
Millennium River Bank Amphitheatre
Maidstone 5H 7
Millennium Way
ME12: S'ness 2B 52
Millen Rd. ME10: Sit 2C 28
Miller Cl. ME10: Kems'y 6E 26
Miller Ct. ME12: Minst 7G 53
Miller Ho. ME15: Maid 5K 7
Millers Wharf ME15: Maid 2G 43
Miller Way ME2: Wain 5A 10
Mill Farm Cotts.
ME3: Hoo W 1G 11
Millfield ME10: Sit 4E 28
Millfields ME5: Lord W 7H 21
Millfordhope Rd. ME2: Strood . . .1E 12
MILLHALL 1A 36
Mill Hall ME20: Aylfd 1A 36
Mill Hall Bus. Est.
ME20: Aylfd 1A 36
Mill Hall Cen. ME20: Aylfd 1A 36
Mill Hall Rd. ME20: Aylfd 1A 36
Mill Hill La. DA12: Shorne 4A 8
Mill La. ME5: Blue H 1B 32
ME5: Chat'm 7G 15
ME6: Snod 2D 30

A-Z Maidstone & Medway Towns 69

Mill La. ME9: H'lip 3A 24
  ME14: Maid 1G 7 (5J 37)
  ME17: Cox 2G 49
  ME18: W'bury 4E 40
Mill Mdw. Yd. ME16: Maid 1G 7
Millpond Cl. ME2: Strood 7K 9
Mill Pond Cotts.
  ME18: W'bury 5E 40
Mill Rd. ME2: Strood 6K 9
  ME7: Gill 3F 5 (2G 15)
Mills Cl. ME12: Minst 6F 53
Mills Rd. ME20: Aylfd 4A 36
Mills Ter. ME4: Chat'm ...6E 4 (5E 14)
Millstock Ter. ME15: Maid 2H 43
MILL STREET 4F 35
Mill St. ME6: Snod 2D 30
  ME10: Sit 2C 28
  ME15: Loose 7J 43
  ME15: Maid 4H 7 (7J 37)
  ME19: E Mal 4G 35
Mill Wlk. ME16: Barm 1D 42
Mill Way ME10: Sit 2D 28
Millwood Ct. ME4: Chat'm 5B 4
Milner Rd. ME7: Gill 1K 5 (1H 15)
Milners ME17: Leeds 6A 46
Milstead Cl. ME12: S'ness 5B 52
  ME14: Maid 6B 38
Milstead Cotts. ME17: Leeds ...6A 46
Milsted Rd. ME8: Gill 6C 16
Milton Av. ME3: Cli W 1A 10
Milton Cl. ME19: Kings H 1C 40
Milton Creek Country Pk. 7E 26
Milton La. ME19: Kings H 1B 40
MILTON REGIS 1C 28
Milton Regis Halt Station
  Sittingbourne & Kemsley
  Light Railway 1E 28
Milton Rd. ME7: Gill 7H 5 (5G 15)
  ME10: Sit 3C 28
Milton St. ME16: Maid 2F 43
Mimosa Av. ME12: Minst 7G 53
Mincers Cl. ME5: Lord W 7G 21
Minerva Rd. ME2: Strood 7J 9
Minor Canon Row
  ME1: Roch 5B 6 (3A 14)
Minor Cen. ME14: Weav 6D 38
MINSTER 6K 53
Minster Abbey
  Church of St Mary
  with St Sexburgha 5K 53
Minster Abbey Gatehouse Mus.
  Sheerness 5K 53
Minster Chalet Pk.
  ME12: Minst 3G 53
Minster Dr. ME12: Minst 4H 53
Minster Rd. ME8: Gill 5C 16
  ME12: Minst 6E 52
Minterne Av. ME10: Sit 5B 28
Miranda Ct. ME12: S'ness 3B 52
Miskin Rd. ME3: Hoo W 2J 11
Mistletoe Dr. ME12: Minst 7H 53
Mitchell Av. ME4: Chat'm 6D 14
Mitchell Rd. ME19: Kings H ...2A 40
Mitre Rd. ME1: Roch ...7A 6 (4K 13)
Moat La. ME2: Upnor 4D 10
Moat Way ME11: Queen 7A 52
MOCKBEGGAR 2J 9
Mockett Ct. ME10: Sit 3C 28
  (off Frederick St.)
Model Cotts. ME1: Burh 2F 31
Monarch Cl. ME5: W'slade 3E 20
  ME15: Maid 3K 43
Monarch Dr. ME10: Kems'y ...5D 26
Monarch Ter. ME19: Kings H ...1D 40
Monckton's Av. ME14: Maid ...4H 37
Monckton's Dr. ME14: Maid ...4H 37
Monckton's La. ME14: Maid ...4H 37
Moncrif Cl. ME14: Bear 7G 39
Monins Rd. ME9: Iwade 3B 26
Monkdown ME15: Bear 3F 45
Monkey Bizz
  Medway City Estate 1C 14
Monkwood Cl. ME1: Roch 1K 19
Monmouth Cl. ME8: Rain 6D 16
Monroe Way ME19: Kings H ...1E 40
Mons Cl. ME10: Kems'y 5D 26
Montague Ct. ME12: S'ness ...3B 52
Montague Ho. ME7: Gill 5J 5
Montfort Dr. ME19: Kings H ...2B 40
Montfort Rd. ME2: Strood 1J 13
  ME5: W'slade 7D 20
Montgomery Av.
  ME12: S'ness 2E 20

Montgomery Rd.
  ME7: Gill 7G 5 (4G 15)
Montpelier Ga. ME16: Alltn 6E 36
Montrose Av. ME5: Chat'm 6J 15
Moonfleet Cl.
  ME10: Kems'y 5E 26
Moonstone Dr. ME5: Lord W ...7F 21
Moonstone Sq. ME10: Sit 1B 28
Moore St. ME2: Strood 7J 9
Mooring Rd. ME1: Roch 7B 14
Moorings, The
  ME15: Maid 6H 7 (1J 43)
Moor Pk. Cl. ME8: Rain 1G 23
MOOR STREET 1H 23
Moor St. ME8: Rain 1H 23
Morden Ct. ME1: Roch 4A 14
Morden St. ME1: Roch ...7B 6 (4A 14)
Morement Rd.
  ME3: Hoo W 1H 11
Morgan Rd. ME2: Strood 7J 9
Morhen Cl. ME6: Snod 3A 30
Morland Dr. ME2: Strood 6J 9
Morlings, The ME14: Bear 7F 39
Morris Cl. ME17: Bou Mo 7C 44
  ME19: E Mal 2G 35
Morris Ct. ME15: Maid 2K 15
Morris Ct. Cl. ME9: Bap 5H 29
Mortimers Av. ME3: Cli W 1A 10
Mortlocks, The ME14: Maid 1J 7
Morton Cl. ME15: Maid 6C 44
Morton St. ME15: Maid 2J 43
Morton Way ME15: Maid 2J 43
Mosquito Rd.
  ME19: Kings H 1A 40
Mossbank ME5: W'slade 6E 20
Mossy Glade ME8: Rain 3E 22
Mostyn Rd. ME14: Maid 7B 38
Mote Av. ME15: Maid 1A 44
Mote Hall Vs. ME14: Bear 7H 39
Mote Ho. ME15: Maid 2D 44
Mote Pk. 2C 44
Mote Rd. ME15: Maid 5K 7 (1K 43)
MOTNEY HILL 3H 17
Motney Hill Rd. ME8: Rain 5G 17
Motney Hill RSPB Reserve 2G 17
Motorway Ind. Est.
  ME20: Aylfd 1F 37
Mouat Ct. ME5: Lord W 6E 20
Mountbatten Av. ME3: High'm ..3E 8
  ME5: Chat'm 2E 20
Mountbatten Pav.
  ME20: Aylfd 3C 36
Mount Cotts. ME8: Bear 7G 39
Mount Dr. ME14: Bear 7G 39
Mount Fld. ME11: Queen 7A 52
Mount La. ME9: H'lip 6K 23
  ME14: Bear 7G 39
Mount Lodge ME1: Roch 6K 13
  (off Valley Vw. Rd.)
Mt. Pleasant ME5: Chat'm 4F 15
  ME20: Aylfd 7J 31
Mt. Pleasant Dr.
  ME14: Bear 6F 39
Mount Rd. ME1: Roch 6J 13
  ME4: Chat'm 7C 4 (5D 14)
Mountsfield Cl. ME16: Maid ...6G 37
Mountview ME9: B'den 7K 25
Mount Vw. Ct. ME4: Chat'm ...6C 4
Moyle Cl. ME8: Parkw 5D 22
Mozart Ct.
  ME4: Chat'm 7A 4 (5C 14)
Muddy La. ME10: Sit 5F 29
Muir Rd. ME15: Maid 6J 7 (2K 43)
Mulberry Cl. ME7: Hpstd 5A 22
Mulberry Ct. ME14: Maid 6A 38
Mulberry Way ME10: Sit 2G 29
Mungean Ho. ME1: Roch 7C 6
Munn's La. ME9: H'lip 3A 24
Munsgore La. ME8: B'den 7G 25
Murrain Dr. ME15: Bear 3F 45
Murray Rd. ME2: Strood 6A 10
MURSTON 3F 29
Murston Rd. ME10: Sit 4F 29
Murthwaite Ct.
  ME12: Minst 7G 53
Museum Av.
  ME14: Maid 2H 7 (6J 37)
Museum St.
  ME14: Maid 3H 7 (7J 37)
Musgrave Rd. ME10: Sit 1D 28
Musket La. ME17: Holl 2B 46
  (not continuous)
Mustang Rd. ME19: Kings H ...1A 40
Mynn Cres. ME14: Bear 7F 39

Myrtle Cres. ME5: W'slade 4D 20
Myrtle Rd. ME12: Minst 7H 53

Nags Head La.
  ME1: Roch 7D 6 (4B 14)
Napier Cl. ME10: Sit 3A 28
Napier Ct. ME14: Maid 4J 37
Napier Rd. ME7: Gill 7J 5 (4H 15)
Napier Ter. ME12: S'ness 2D 52
  (off Marine Pde.)
Napwood Cl. ME8: Parkw 3D 22
Nares Rd. ME8: Parkw 5D 22
Nash Cl. ME5: Lord W 7G 21
Nashenden Down
  Local Nature Reserve 2J 19
Nashenden Farm La.
  ME1: Roch 7H 13
Nashenden La. ME1: Roch 6H 13
Natal Rd.
  ME4: Chat'm 7D 4 (5E 14)
Nativity Cl. ME10: Sit 3C 28
Nautilus Cl. ME12: Minst 7G 53
Nautilus Dr. ME12: Minst 7G 53
Naval Ter. ME12: S'ness 1A 52
Naylor's Cotts. ME7: B'hst 7B 22
Neale St. ME4: Chat'm ...7C 4 (6D 14)
Neath Ct. ME15: Maid 4D 44
Neighbourhood Cen.
  ME5: W'slade 3F 21
Nelson Av. ME12: Minst 6K 53
Nelson Cl. ME12: S'ness 4A 52
Nelson Ct. ME5: Chat'm 7H 15
Nelson Est. ME7: Gill 6J 5 (4H 15)
Nelson Ho. ME15: Maid 7E 44
Nelson Rd. ME1: Woul 5C 18
  ME7: Gill 6J 5 (4H 15)
Nelson Ter. ME5: Chat'm 7G 15
  ME8: Gill 5H 5
Nelson Wlk. ME10: Sit 4K 25
Neptune Bus. Pk. ME2: Med E ..1C 14
Neptune Cl.
  ME2: Med E 1A 4 (1C 14)
Neptune Ter. ME2: S'ness 2D 52
Neptune Way ME2: Med E 2C 14
Nestor Ct. ME18: Tstn 4H 41
Nethermount ME14: Bear 7G 39
Netley Cl. ME14: Maid 5C 38
NETTLESTEAD 6E 40
Nettlestead La.
  ME18: W'bury 6B 40
Nettle Way ME12: Minst 7H 53
Nevill Cl. ME19: W Mal 2D 34
Neville Cl. ME14: Pen H 3A 38
Neville Rd. ME4: Chat'm 6C 14
Nevill Pl. ME6: Snod 3C 30
Nevill Rd. ME6: Snod 3C 30
Newark Ct. ME2: Strood 1K 13
Newark Yd.
  ME2: Strood 2A 6 (1K 13)
New Barns Rd. ME14: Pen H ...3K 37
Newbridge Av. ME10: Sit 7C 26
Newbury Av. ME16: Alltn 4F 37
Newbury Cl. ME3: Cli W 1A 10
Newchurch Rd. ME15: Maid ...3K 43
Newcomen Rd. ME12: S'ness ..2C 52
New Cotts. ME9: Rod 7D 28
  ME9: Tonge 6J 29
  ME15: Hunt 3B 48
New Covenant Pl.
  ME1: Roch 7E 6 (4B 14)
New Cut ME4: Chat'm 4B 4 (4D 14)
  ME15: E Far 5G 43
New Cut Rd. ME14: Weav 7C 38
Newenden Cl. ME14: Maid 5B 38
Newenden Rd. ME2: Wain 5A 10
NEW HYTHE 6D 30
New Hythe Bus. Pk.
  ME20: Lark 7D 30
New Hythe La. ME20: Lark 2H 35
New Hythe Station (Rail) 6E 30
NEWINGTON 3D 24
Newington Ct. ME9: N'tn 3F 25
Newington Ent. Cen.
  ME9: N'tn 1E 24
Newington Ind. Est.
  ME9: N'tn 1E 24
Newington Station (Rail) 3D 24
Newington Wlk. ME14: Maid ...5B 38
New Inn Cotts. ME15: E Far ...5F 43
  (off Forge La.)
Newitt Rd. ME3: Hoo W 2J 11

New Kent Rd. ME4: Chat'm 7F 11
Newland Rd. ME12: S'ness 5A 52
Newlands Av. ME10: Sit 5K 25
Newlyn Ct.
  ME14: Maid 3K 7 (7K 37)
Newman Dr. ME10: Kems'y 6D 26
Newnham Cl. ME8: Gill 6C 16
Newnham Ct. Shop. Village
  ME14: Weav 4D 38
Newnham St. ME4: Chat'm 5F 15
New Rd. ME1: Burh 1H 31
  ME1: Roch 7D 6 (4B 14)
  ME4: Chat'm
  ....5B 4 & 4A 4 (4D 14)
  ME12: Minst 6J 53
  ME12: S'ness 4A 52
  ME17: L'ly 6H 45
  ME19: E Mal 3H 35
  ME20: Dit 2K 35
New Rd. Av.
  ME4: Chat'm 4A 4 (4C 14)
New Rd. Ind. Est.
  ME12: S'ness 3A 52
New Stairs
  ME4: Chat'm 1B 4 (2D 14)
New St. ME4: Chat'm ...6A 4 (5C 14)
  ME12: S'ness 3B 52
Newton Cl. ME5: Lord W 7G 21
  ME16: Maid 1H 43
NEW TOWN
  ME2 ....3C 18
  ME19 ....3B 34
New Villas ME15: E Far 5F 43
NHS WALK-IN CENTRE
  Maidstone 7D 36
  (within Maidstone Hospital)
Niagara Cl. ME19: Kings H 1C 40
Nicholas Cl. ME16: Barm 1D 42
Nicklaus Dr. ME5: W'slade 6D 20
Nickleby Cl. ME1: Roch 6A 14
Nightingale Cl. ME8: Rain 3E 22
  ME20: Lark 1G 35
Nightingale Ct. ME2: Strood ...2E 12
Nightingale Ho. ME1: Roch 4C 14
  (off St Bartholomew's La.)
Nile Rd. ME7: Gill 6H 5 (4G 15)
Nimbus Ent. Pk. ME16: Alltn ...3F 37
Nine Acres Rd. ME2: Cux 5D 12
Niven Cl. ME3: Wain 4A 10
Niwrim Way ME12: Minst 3G 53
Nobbys Gym
  Milton Regis 1C 28
NOKE STREET 3A 10
Nora La. ME3: High'm 3D 8
Nore Cl. ME7: Gill 7J 15
  ME2: S'ness 3C 52
Noreen Av. ME12: Minst 6G 53
Norfolk Cl. ME5: Lord W 6G 21
  ME8: Rain 6D 16
Norfolk Rd. ME15: Maid 4B 44
Norman Cl. ME2: Strood 4H 13
  ME8: Wigm 5B 22
  ME14: Maid 5A 38
Norman Rd. ME6: Snod 4C 30
  ME19: W Mal 2B 34
Normanwood Ct.
  ME12: S'ness 2D 52
  (off Unity St.)
Nor Marsh RSPB Reserve 1D 16
Norrington Rd. ME15: Maid ...6K 43
Northbank Ho. ME2: Med E ...2B 14
Northbourne Rd. ME8: Gill 4B 16
Northcote Rd. ME2: Strood 1J 13
North Cl. ME15: Maid 3K 43
North Cres. ME17: Cox 1G 49
Nth. Dane Way
  ME5: Chat'm, Lord W 2G 21
Northdown Cl. ME14: Pen H ...4A 38
Nth. Downs Ho. ME2: Hall'g ...4A 18
Northfields ME16: Barm 2C 42
Northfleet Cl. ME14: Maid 6B 38
Nth. Folly Rd. ME15: E Far 2C 48
Northgate ME1: Roch 4C 6 (2A 14)
NORTH HALLING 1C 18
Northleigh Cl. ME15: Maid 6K 43
North Lockside Rd.
  ME4: Chat'm 7H 11
Northpoint Bus. Est.
  ME2: Med E 7B 10
  (off Enterprise Cl.)

Quarry Cotts.—Romany Rd.

Quarry Cotts. ME17: Bou Mo 1A 50
Quarry Rd. ME15: Maid . . .7J 7 (2K 43)
Quarry Sq.
ME14: Maid 1K 7 (6K 37)
QUARRY WOOD 3B 36
Quarry Wood Ind. Est.
ME20: Aylfd 3B 36
Quarry Wood Nature Reserve
. . . . .1A 48
Quartz Way ME10: Sit 1A 28
Quayside ME4: Chat'm 6F 11
(not continuous)
Queen Anne Rd.
ME14: Maid 3K 7 (7K 37)
QUEENBOROUGH 7A 52
Queenborough Dr.
ME12: Minst 5H 53
Queenborough Rd.
ME12: Minst 7B 52
(not continuous)
Queenborough Station (Rail) . . .7A 52
Queendown Av. ME8: Parkw 4D 22
QUEEN DOWN WARREN 7H 23
Queendown Warren Nature Reserve
. . . . .6H 23
Queen Elizabeth Sq.
ME15: Maid 6C 44
Queen Mother Court, The
ME1: Roch 4K 13
Queen's Av. ME6: Snod 2C 30
ME16: Maid 6G 37
Queen's Farm Rd.
DA12: Shorne, Grav'nd 1A 8
Queensgate ME16: Maid 6G 37
Queens Ho. ME16: Maid 1E 42
Queens Own Royal
West Kent Regiment Mus.
. . . .*2H 7*
(within Maidstone Mus.)
Queens Pde. ME12: S'ness 4A 52
Queens Rd. ME5: Chat'm 6H 15
ME6: Snod 2C 30
ME7: Gill 6H 5 (4G 15)
ME12: Minst 5K 53
ME16: Maid 1E 42
Queen St. ME1: Roch 7C 6 (4A 14)
(not continuous)
ME4: Chat'm 4D 4 (4E 14)
ME19: Kings H 1C 40
Queen's Way ME12: S'ness 4A 52
Queensway ME14: Det 2F 39
Queenswood Rd. ME20: Aylfd . . .3B 32
Quern, The ME15: Maid 3H 43
Quested Way ME17: H'shm 6K 47
Quickstep Cl. ME10: Sit 6D 26
Quickthorn Cres.
ME5: Chat'm 4C 20
Quindell Pl. ME19: Kings H 1D 40
Quinion Cl. ME5: W'slade 2D 32
Quinnell St. ME8: Rain 7E 16
Quinton Rd. ME10: Sit 7A 26
Quixote Cres. ME2: Strood 6K 9

R

Racefield Cl. DA12: Shorne 6A 8
RADFIELD 5K 29
Radleigh Gdns. ME1: Roch 7C 14
Radnor Cl. ME14: Maid 5J 37
Raggatt Pl. ME15: Maid 2A 44
Ragstone Ct. ME20: Dit 3K 35
Ragstone Flds.
ME17: Bou Mo 1D 50
Ragstone Rd. ME15: Bear 2F 45
Railway Rd. ME12: S'ness 2B 52
Railway St.
ME4: Chat'm 5B 4 (4D 14)
(not continuous)
ME7: Gill 4J 5 (3H 15)
Railway St. Ind. Est.
ME7: Gill 3K 5 (2H 15)
Railway Ter. ME11: Queen 7A 52
RAINHAM 1F 23
Rainham Cl. ME15: Maid 3K 43
Rainham Rd. ME5: Chat'm 5G 15
ME7: Gill 5G 15
Rainham Shop. Cen.
ME8: Rain 7F 17
Rainham Station (Rail) 7F 17
Raite Grn. ME10: Sit 1B 28
Raleigh Cl. ME5: W'slade 3E 20
Raleigh Way ME12: Minst 6E 52
Ramillies Cl. ME5: W'slade 3E 20
Rampion Cl. ME14: Weav 6D 38
Ramsey Cl. ME15: Maid 2K 43
Randall Rd. ME4: Chat'm 7C 14
Randalls Row ME15: Loose 7J 43
Randall St.
ME14: Maid 1H 7 (5J 37)
Randle Way ME9: Bap 5J 29
Randolph Cotts. ME2: Strood 6K 9
Randolph Ho.
ME7: Gill 5H 5 (3G 15)
Randolph Rd.
ME7: Gill 5H 5 (3G 15)
Ranelagh Rd. ME12: S'ness 2C 52
Ranscombe Cl. ME2: Strood 3F 13
Ranscombe Farm Reserve 3D 12
Raspberry Hill La.
ME9: Iwade 1A 26
Ratcliffe Highway
ME3: Hoo W 2E 10
Raven Cl. ME20: Lark 2H 35
Raven Knowle ME1: Woul 5F 19
Ravensbourne Ho.
ME2: Strood 4G 13
Ravens Dane Cl. ME15: Bear 3F 45
Ravenswood Av. ME2: Strood 7K 9
Rawdon Rd.
ME15: Maid 6K 7 (1K 43)
Rayfield Ct. ME6: Snod 1C 30
Rayleigh Cl. ME16: Alltn 4G 37
Raymer Rd. ME14: Pen H 3A 38
Readers Ct. ME18: Tstn 4H 41
Reading Ho. ME15: Maid 7E 44
Readscroft Rd. ME8: Parkw 4D 22
Realgar Ct. ME10: Sit 1B 28
Reams Way ME10: Kems'y 5E 26
Recreation Av. ME6: Snod 2C 30
Recreation Cl. ME14: Maid 5A 38
Recreation Way
ME10: Kems'y 5D 26
Rectory Cl. ME1: Woul 4E 18
ME6: Snod 2C 30
Rectory Grange ME1: Roch 6K 13
Rectory La. ME16: Maid 3C 42
ME17: Cha S 7H 51
ME17: Sut V 6K 51
Rectory La. Nth. ME19: Leyb 1F 35
Rectory La. Sth. ME19: Leyb 1F 35
Rectory Rd. ME10: Sit 4F 29
Reculver Wlk. ME15: Maid 5E 44
Red Admiral Cres.
ME9: Iwade 2B 26
Redan Pl. ME12: S'ness 2D 52
Redbank ME19: Leyb 1F 35
Redbridge Cl. ME5: Lord W 5F 21
Redcliffe La. ME14: Pen H 4A 38
Red Cotts. ME16: Alltn 3H 37
Rede Ct. Rd. ME2: Strood 7F 9
Redfe Wood Rd. ME16: Barm 1B 42
Redfern Av. ME7: Gill 3J 15
RED HILL 3G 41
Red Hill ME18: E Mal, W'bury . . .2G 41
Red Ho. Gdns. ME18: W'bury . . .5D 40
Redland Shaw ME1: Roch 7C 14
Redruth Mnr. ME7: Gill 3G 5
Redsells Cl. ME15: Bear 3F 45
Redshank Rd. ME4: St Mary 6E 10
Redvers Rd.
ME4: Chat'm 7D 4 (6E 14)
Redwall Bungs. ME17: Lint 7G 49
Redwall La. ME15: Hunt 6D 48
ME17: Lint 6D 48
Redwell Gro. ME19: Kings H 2D 40
Redwing Av. ME9: Iwade 2C 26
Redwing Cl. ME20: Lark 7B 30
Redwing Rd. ME5: W'slade 3F 21
Redwood Cl. ME5: W'slade 7F 21
Redwood Glade ME7: B'hst 7A 22
Reed Cl. ME20: Lark 6C 30
Reedham Cres. ME3: Cli W 2B 10
Reeves Ct. ME19: E Mal 2H 35
Reform Rd. ME4: Chat'm 5F 15
Regency Cl. ME8: Wigm 6C 22
ME12: S'ness 1A 52
Regency Ct. ME10: Sit 3B 28
Regent Bus. Cen.
ME5: Lord W 1G 33
Regent Cl. ME15: Maid 3K 43
Regent Dr. ME15: Maid 4K 43
Regent Ho. ME2: Strood 1A 6
Regent Rd. ME7: Gill 6F 5 (4G 15)
Regents Pl. *ME12: S'ness 2B 52*
(off High St.)
Regent Way ME19: Kings H 7D 34
Reginald Av. ME2: Cux 5E 12
Reginald Rd.
ME16: Maid 6F 7 (1H 43)
Regis Bus. Pk. ME12: S'ness . . .3A 52
Regis Cres. ME10: Sit 1C 28
Regis Ind. Est. ME12: S'ness . . .4A 52
Reinden Gro. ME15: Bear 3E 44
Renown Rd. ME5: Lord W 7G 21
Repton Way ME5: W'slade 5D 20
Reservoir Cotts. ME2: Hall'g 5A 18
Resolution Cl. ME5: W'slade 3E 20
Restharrow Rd. ME14: Weav 7D 38
Restharrow Way
ME4: St Mary 6G 11
Restoration House
Rochester 6C 6
Retreat Caravan Park, The
ME18: W'bury 6E 40
Rettendon Dr. ME10: Sit 6D 26
Revenge Rd. ME5: Lord W 1G 33
Reynolds Flds. ME3: High'm 1E 8
Rhode Ct. ME10: Sit 2A 28
Rhodes Ho. *ME5: Chat'm 6G 15*
(off Beacon Hill)
Rhode St. ME4: Chat'm . . .5C 4 (4E 14)
Rhodewood Cl. ME15: Bear 3F 45
Richard St. ME1: Roch 5A 14
ME4: Chat'm 5C 4 (4D 14)
Richard Watts Ct. ME4: Chat'm . . .3B 4
Richborough Dr. ME2: Strood 6J 9
Richmond Av. ME19: Kings H . . .1C 40
Richmond Cl. ME2: Upnor 6D 10
ME5: Lord W 5F 21
Richmond Dr. ME10: Sit 7C 26
Richmond Rd.
ME7: Gill 2H 5 (2G 15)
Richmond St. ME12: S'ness 3D 52
Richmond Way ME15: Maid 4K 43
Riddles Rd. ME9: Sit 4A 28
ME10: Sit 4A 28
Ridgepoint Ct. ME14: Maid 1K 7
Ridgeway, The DA12: Shorne 6A 8
ME4: Chat'm 2C 20
ME7: Gill 1H 5 (1G 15)
Ridgeway Bungs.
DA12: Shorne 6B 8
Ridgway ME16: Maid 2E 42
Ridham Av. ME10: Kems'y 5D 26
Ridham Dock ME9: Iwade 1F 27
Ridley Rd. ME1: Roch 7A 6 (4K 13)
Rigden's Ct. ME10: Sit 2C 28
Riggall Ct. ME2: Cux 6C 12
Rileys Pk. Dr. ME2: Strood 4G 13
RINGLESTONE 4J 37
Ringlestone Cres.
ME14: Maid 3J 37
Ringlet Gro. ME9: Iwade 3B 26
Ringlet Rd. ME4: St Mary 5F 11
Ringwood Cl. ME8: Gill 1D 22
Ringwood Rd. ME15: Maid 4B 44
Ripon Cl. ME8: Rain 5D 16
Ripton Cotts. ME18: Tstn 5H 41
Rise, The ME1: Roch 5B 14
ME4: Chat'm 1E 14
ME7: Hpstd 6A 22
ME9: B'den 7K 25
ME12: Minst 7C 52
Ritch Rd. ME6: Snod 2A 30
Rivenhall Ct. ME3: Hoo W 1J 11
Rivenhall Way ME3: Hoo W 1J 11
River Bank Cl. ME15: Maid 7A 38
Riverbank Pk. ME12: Minst 3G 53
Riverbourne Ct. ME10: Sit 4D 28
River Cl. ME15: E Far 5D 42
River Dr. ME2: Strood 1G 13
Riverhead Cl. ME10: Sit 4A 28
ME16: Alltn 5G 37
Rivermead ME4: St Mary 5G 11
Rivers Cl. ME18: W'bury 5F 41
Riverside ME2: Strood . . .1C 6 (1A 14)
ME4: Chat'm 3B 4 (3D 14)
Riverside Bus. Pk.
ME20: Lark 5E 30
Riverside Caravan Pk.
ME16: E Far 4D 42
Riverside Country Pk. 3C 16
Riverside Country Pk. Vis. Cen.
. . . . .3D 16
Riverside E. Rd. ME4: Chat'm . . .5G 11
Riverside Est.
ME2: Med E 1A 4 (2C 14)
Riverside Vw. ME20: Aylfd 1E 36
Riverside Wlk. ME15: Maid 5H 7
River St. ME7: Gill 2E 14
River Vw. ME8: Gill 5D 16
ME15: Maid 7H 7 (2J 43)
River Vw. Cl.
ME4: Chat'm 7B 4 (5D 14)
River Way ME20: Lark 6C 30
Roach St. ME2: Strood 1J 13
Roan Ct. ME2: Strood 7H 9
Robert Bean Lodge
ME1: Roch 7C 14
Roberts Cl. ME10: Sit 7B 26
Roberts Orchard Rd.
ME16: Barm 1C 42
Roberts Rd. ME6: Snod 2B 30
ME8: Gill 1E 22
Robin Ct. ME1: Roch 7E 6
Robin Hood La. ME5: W'slade . . .7D 20
Robin Hood La. (Lower)
ME5: W'slade 1C 32
Robin Hood La. (Upper)
ME5: Blue H 1B 32
Robin Ho. ME16: Maid . . .4F 7 (7H 37)
Robins Ct. ME14: Pen H 4A 38
Robson Dr. ME3: Hoo W 2H 11
ME20: Aylfd 1A 36
Rocfort Rd. ME6: Snod 2C 30
ROCHESTER 5C 6 (3A 14)
ROCHESTER AIRPORT 4A 20
Rochester Airport
(Park & Ride) 2B 20
Rochester Airport Ind. Est.
ME1: Roch 3A 20
Rochester & Cobham Pk. Golf Course
. . . . .2A 12
Rochester Av.
ME1: Roch 7C 6 (4A 14)
Rochester Castle 4B 6 (2A 14)
Rochester Cathedral 5C 6 (2A 14)
Rochester Ct. ME2: Med E 7B 10
Rochester Cres. ME3: Hoo W . . .1H 11
Rochester Cruising Club
. . . . .4A 6 (2K 13)
Rochester Ga. ME1: Roch 6D 6
Rochester Health Club 2A 20
Rochester Ho. ME15: Maid 5C 44
Rochester Rd.
ME1: Burh, Woul 5F 19
ME1: Roch 3A 20
ME2: Cux 7D 12
ME5: Chat'm 3A 20
ME20: Aylfd 7J 31
Rochester Station (Rail)
. . . . .6E 6 (3B 14)
Rochester St.
ME4: Chat'm 7A 4 (6C 14)
Rock Av. ME7: Gill 7H 5 (4G 15)
Rock Ho. ME16: Maid 4F 7
Rocklands ME16: Maid 5F 7
Rock Rd. ME10: Sit 3C 28
ME14: Pen H 4K 37
Rocks Cl. ME19: E Mal 5H 35
Rocks Road, The
ME19: E Mal 5H 35
Rockwell Ct. ME15: Maid 3H 43
Rocky Hill ME16: Maid . . .4F 7 (7H 37)
Rocky Hill Ter.
ME16: Maid 4F 7 (7H 37)
Rodmer Cl. ME12: Minst 4J 53
RODMERSHAM 7H 29
RODMERSHAM GREEN 7F 29
Rodmersham Grn. ME9: Rod 7F 29
Roebuck Bus. Pk.
ME17: H'shm 6K 47
Roebuck Ho. *ME1: Roch 4B 14*
(off Doust Way)
Roebuck Rd.
ME1: Roch 6B 6 (3A 14)
Roffen Rd. ME1: Roch 6A 14
Roko Health Club 6A 16
Roland Ho. *ME15: Maid 3H 43*
(off Harris Pl.)
Rolvenden Av. ME8: Gill 5C 16
Rolvenden Dr. ME10: Sit 4K 25
Rolvenden Rd. ME2: Wain 5A 10
Roman Cl. ME5: Blue H 1B 32
Roman Hgts. ME14: Maid 5B 38
Roman Rd. ME6: Snod 2B 30
Roman Sq. ME10: Sit 4D 28
Roman Way ME2: Strood 4H 13
ME17: Bou Mo 1D 50
Romany Ct. ME5: Chat'm 6H 15
Romany Rd. ME8: Gill 6B 16

A-Z Maidstone & Medway Towns 73

Rome Ter.—Sandy La.

Rome Ter. ME4: Chat'm . . . 4B 4 (4D 14)
Romney Cl. ME14: Bear . . . 1F 45
Romney Ct. ME10: Sit . . . 2B 28
Romney Pl. ME15: Maid . . . 4K 7 (7K 37)
Romney Rd. ME5: W'slade . . . 4F 21
Romsey Cl. ME2: Strood . . . 7G 9
Ronalds Ct. ME10: Sit . . . 3E 28
Rookery Vw. ME9: Iwade . . . 2B 26
Rook La. ME9: Bob . . . 3G 25
Rooks Vw. ME9: Bob . . . 3G 25
Roonagh Ct. ME10: Sit . . . 5C 28
Roosevelt Av. ME5: Chat'm . . . 2D 20
Ropemakers Ct. ME4: Chat'm . . . 7E 14
Roper Cl. ME8: Parkw . . . 6C 22
Roper's La. ME3: Hoo W . . . 1K 11
Rope Wlk. ME4: Chat'm . . . 3C 4 (3D 14)
ROSEACRE . . . 7F 39
Roseacre Gdns. ME14: Bear . . . 7F 39
Roseacre La. ME14: Bear . . . 1F 45
Rosebery Cl. ME10: Sit . . . 3H 29
Rosebery Rd. ME4: Chat'm . . . 6C 14
ME7: Gill . . . 1J 5 (1H 15)
Rose Cotts. ME2: Strood . . . 7D 8
Rose Ct. ME17: Lint . . . 4G 49
Roseholme ME16: Maid . . . 2G 43
Rose Jolley Ct. ME7: Gill . . . 5J 5 (3H 15)
Roseleigh Av. ME16: Alltn . . . 7F 37
Roseleigh Rd. ME10: Sit . . . 6B 28
Rosemary Av. ME12: Minst . . . 6D 52
Rosemary Cl. ME5: W'slade . . . 5D 20
Rosemary Ct. ME1: Roch . . . 7D 6
Rosemary Gdns. ME15: Maid . . . 7D 44
Rosemary Rd. ME15: Bear . . . 1F 45
ME19: E Mal . . . 2G 35
Rosemount Cl. ME15: Loose . . . 1J 49
Rosemount Ct. ME2: Strood . . . 6J 9
Rosemount Gdns. ME14: Weav . . . 7D 38
Rose St. ME1: Roch . . . 5B 14
ME12: S'ness . . . 2B 52
Rose Wlk. ME10: Sit . . . 5D 28
Rose Yd. ME14: Maid . . . 3J 7 (7K 37)
Rosslyn Grn. ME16: Alltn . . . 6E 36
Ross St. ME1: Roch . . . 7D 6 (4B 14)
Rotary Gdns. ME7: Gill . . . 6K 15
Rother Vale ME5: Lord W . . . 6G 21
Rougemont ME19: Kings H . . . 2D 40
Roughetts Rd. ME19: Rya . . . 1A 34
Roundel, The ME10: Sit . . . 5D 28
Roundel Cl. ME19: Kings H . . . 7E 34
Roundels, The ME9: Lyn . . . 7K 29
Roundhay ME19: Leyb . . . 2E 34
Roundwell ME14: Bear . . . 7J 39
Round Wood Cl. ME5: W'slade . . . 1E 32
Rover Rd. ME5: Lord W . . . 7F 21
Rowan Cl. ME20: Aylfd . . . 2B 36
Rowan Ho. *ME5: W'slade . . . 4D 20*
(off Gorse Av.)
ME16: Barm . . . 1C 42
Rowan Lea ME5: Chat'm . . . 7F 15
Rowans, The ME12: Minst . . . 5H 53
Rowan Wlk. ME4: Chat'm . . . 6A 4 (5C 14)
Rowbrocke Cl. ME8: Parkw . . . 6D 22
Rowe Pl. ME20: Eccl . . . 4H 31
Rowland Av. ME7: Gill . . . 6J 15
Rowland Cl. ME7: Gill . . . 7J 15
ME16: Maid . . . 5F 7 (1H 43)
ROYAL BRITISH LEGION VILLAGE . . . 3D 36
Royal Ct. ME12: S'ness . . . 2C 52
Royal Eagle Cl. ME2: Med E . . . 1C 14
Royal Engineers Mus. . . . 1F 15
Royal Engineers Rd. ME14: S'lng, Maid . . . 1H 7 (2H 37)
Royal Fountain M. *ME12: S'ness . . . 2A 52*
(off West St.)
Royal Rd. ME12: S'ness . . . 2C 52
Royal Sovereign Av. ME4: Chat'm . . . 1F 5 (1F 15)
Royal Star Arc. ME14: Maid . . . 3H 7 (7J 37)
Roydon Hall Rd. TN12: E Peck . . . 7A 40
Royston Rd. ME15: Bear . . . 1F 45
Roystons Cl. ME8: Rain . . . 6F 17
Rubin Pl. ME19: Kings H . . . 1C 40
Ruby Cl. ME10: Sit . . . 1B 28
Ruby Wlk. ME19: Kings H . . . 1D 40
Ruckinge Way ME8: Gill . . . 5C 16
Rudge Cl. ME5: Lord W . . . 7H 21
Rugby Cl. ME5: W'slade . . . 5D 20
Ruins Barn Rd. ME10: T'stall . . . 7B 28
Rule Ct. ME12: S'ness . . . 4B 52
Rumwood Ct. ME17: L'ly . . . 7H 45
Runcie Cl. ME15: Maid . . . 2J 43
Running Horse Rdbt. ME14: S'lng . . . 2H 37
Runnymede Gdns. ME15: Maid . . . 4K 43
Rush Cl. ME5: W'slade . . . 6E 20
Rushdean Rd. ME2: Strood . . . 3F 13
Rushenden Rd. ME11: Queen . . . 7A 52
Rushes, The ME20: Lark . . . 6D 30
Rushmead Dr. ME15: Maid . . . 5K 43
Ruskin Cl. ME19: E Mal . . . 3G 35
Ruskin Gro. ME15: Maid . . . 6C 44
Russell Cl. ME10: Sit . . . 4A 28
Russell Ct. ME4: Chat'm . . . 5F 15
Russell Rd. ME20: Aylfd . . . 3B 32
Russell's Av. ME8: Rain . . . 1G 23
Russell St. ME12: S'ness . . . 2B 52
(not continuous)
Russet Cl. ME2: Strood . . . 7G 9
Russet Ct. ME17: Cox . . . 2F 49
Russets, The ME16: Alltn . . . 6E 36
Russett Cl. ME20: Aylfd . . . 3B 36
Russett Farm ME8: Rain . . . 5D 16
Russet Way ME19: Kings H . . . 2A 40
Ruth Ho. ME16: Maid . . . 2F 7 (6H 37)
Ruth St. ME4: Chat'm . . . 7E 4 (6E 14)
Rutland Cotts. ME17: Leeds . . . 7K 45
Rutland Pl. ME8: Wigm . . . 6C 22
Rutland Way ME15: Maid . . . 4D 44
Ryan Dr. ME15: Bear . . . 2F 45
Ryarsh La. ME19: W Mal . . . 2C 34
Rycault Cl. ME16: Maid . . . 5F 7 (1H 43)
Rycaut Cl. ME8: Parkw . . . 6D 22
Rydal Ho. ME15: Maid . . . 5C 44
Ryde Cl. ME5: Chat'm . . . 1F 21
Ryegrass Cl. ME5: Lord W . . . 3G 21

S

Sabre Ct. ME8: Gill . . . 7A 16
Saddlers Cl. ME14: Weav . . . 6D 38
Sadlers Cl. ME5: Blue H . . . 7B 20
Saffron Cl. ME16: Maid . . . 1E 42
Saffron Way ME5: W'slade . . . 4D 20
ME10: Sit . . . 7D 26
Sage Ct. ME16: Maid . . . 1D 42
Sage Rd. ME1: Roch . . . 5J 13
Sail Fld. Ct. ME4: Chat'm . . . 1E 14
Sailmakers Ct. ME4: Chat'm . . . 6F 15
St Agnes Gdns. ME12: S'ness . . . 3C 52
St Albans Cl. ME7: Gill . . . 1J 15
St Alban's Rd. ME2: Strood . . . 2F 13
St Albans Wlk. ME4: Chat'm . . . 6A 4 (5C 14)
St Andrew's Cl. ME16: Maid . . . 2D 42
St Andrews Pk. ME16: Maid . . . 1D 42
St Andrews Rd. ME7: Gill . . . 1J 5 (1H 15)
ME16: Maid . . . 2D 42
St Annes Ct. ME16: Maid . . . 3F 7 (7H 37)
St Asaph Ho. ME15: Maid . . . 5C 44
St Barnabas Cl. ME7: Gill . . . 7K 5 (5H 15)
ME16: Alltn . . . 3F 37
ST BARTHOLOMEW'S HOSPITAL . . . 4C 14
St Bartholomew's La. ME1: Roch . . . 4C 14
St Bartholomews Ter. ME1: Roch . . . 4C 14
St Benedict Rd. ME6: Snod . . . 3A 30
St Catherine's Gdns. *ME15: Maid . . . 6C 44*
(off St Catherine's Rd.)
St Catherines Hospital ME1: Roch . . . 7D 6 (4B 14)
St Catherine's Rd. ME15: Maid . . . 6C 44
St Clement's Ho. ME1: Roch . . . 5D 6 (3B 14)
St Davids Ga. ME16: Barm . . . 2D 42
St David's Ho. ME15: Maid . . . 5C 44
St Edmunds Way ME8: Rain . . . 7G 17
St Faiths Ct. ME14: Bear . . . 7G 39
St Faith's La. ME14: Bear . . . 7G 39
St Faith's St. ME14: Maid . . . 3H 7 (7J 37)
St Francis Cl. ME2: Strood . . . 2G 13
ME14: Pen H . . . 4A 38
St George's Av. ME12: S'ness . . . 4B 52
St Georges Bus. Pk. ME10: Sit . . . 3F 29
St Georges Ct. ME12: S'ness . . . 4B 52
St George's Rd. ME7: Gill . . . 2H 5 (2G 15)
St George's Sq. ME16: Maid . . . 1G 43
ST HELENS CORNER . . . 5B 42
St Helen's Cotts. ME15: E Far . . . 4B 42
St Helens La. ME15: E Far . . . 4B 42
St Helen's Rd. ME12: S'ness . . . 3C 52
St Helier's Cl. ME16: Maid . . . 2E 42
St James Cl. ME19: E Mal . . . 3G 35
St James Ct. ME7: Gill . . . 3H 5
St John's Av. ME10: Sit . . . 4F 29
St John's Cl. ME3: High'm . . . 3E 8
St Johns Rd. ME3: High'm . . . 3E 8
ME3: Hoo W . . . 1H 11
ME7: Gill . . . 5G 15
St Johns Way ME1: Roch . . . 6J 13
(not continuous)
St Katherine Rd. ME12: Minst . . . 5E 52
St Katherine's La. ME6: Snod . . . 3B 30
St Laurence Av. ME16: Alltn . . . 3E 36
St Laurence Cl. ME9: Bap . . . 5H 29
St Leonards Av. ME4: Chat'm . . . 6D 14
St Leonards Rd. ME16: Alltn . . . 3F 37
ST LEONARD'S STREET . . . 5C 34
St Leonard's St. ME19: W Mal . . . 5B 34
St Leonard's Tower . . . 4C 34
St Lukes Av. ME14: Maid . . . 6A 38
St Luke's Ct. ME14: Maid . . . 1K 7
St Lukes Rd. ME14: Maid . . . 1K 7 (6A 38)
St Margaret's Banks ME1: Roch . . . 6D 6 (3B 14)
(not continuous)
St Margaret's Cl. ME16: Maid . . . 2E 42
St Margarets Dr. ME8: Wigm . . . 4C 22
St Margaret's M. ME1: Roch . . . 5B 6 (3A 14)
St Margaret's St. ME1: Roch . . . 7A 6 (4K 13)
St Mark's Cl. ME9: N'tn . . . 2E 24
St Marks Ct. ME20: Eccl . . . 4H 31
St Mark's Ho's. ME7: Gill . . . 4G 5 (3G 15)
St Martin's Cl. ME9: N'tn . . . 2E 24
ME14: Det . . . 2F 39
St Mary's Abbey . . . 3D 34
St Mary's Ct. ME19: W Mal . . . 3C 34
St Mary's Gdns. ME4: Chat'm . . . 1F 15
ST MARY'S ISLAND . . . 6G 11
St Mary's Rd. ME2: Strood . . . 1A 6 (1K 13)
ME7: Gill . . . 2H 5 (2G 15)
St Mary's Row ME12: Minst . . . 6G 53
St Mary's Vw. ME9: N'tn . . . 2E 24
St Mary's Wlk. ME1: Burh . . . 1H 31
St Matthew's Cl. ME9: N'tn . . . 2E 24
St Matthews Dr. ME1: Roch . . . 6J 13
St Michaels Cl. ME4: Chat'm . . . 6B 4 (5D 14)
ME10: Sit . . . 3D 28
ME20: Aylfd . . . 7A 32
St Michaels Ct. ME2: Strood . . . 1A 6 (7K 9)
St Michael's Rd. ME10: Sit . . . 3C 28
ME16: Maid . . . 1G 43
St Nicholas Gdns. ME2: Strood . . . 1H 13
St Patricks Row *ME9: Rod . . . 7F 29*
(off Rodmersham Grn.)
St Paul's Cl. ME2: Strood . . . 3F 13
St Paul's St. ME10: Sit . . . 2C 28
(not continuous)
St Peter's Bri. ME14: Maid . . . 4G 7 (7J 37)
St Peter's Cl. ME12: Minst . . . 6D 52
ME20: Dit . . . 2J 35
St Peter's Ct. ME20: Dit . . . 2J 35
St Peter's Path *ME1: Roch . . . 7D 6*
(off King St.)
St Peter's Pl. ME20: Eccl . . . 4H 31
St Peter's Rd. ME20: Dit . . . 2J 35
St Peter's St. ME16: Maid . . . 2G 7 (6J 37)
St Peter St. ME1: Roch . . . 7D 6 (4B 14)
St Philip's Av. ME15: Maid . . . 6K 7 (1A 44)
St Ronans Cl. ME15: Maid . . . 5B 44
St Saviours Rd. ME15: Maid . . . 6C 44
St Stephen's Cl. ME9: N'tn . . . 2E 24
St Stephen's Cotts. ME15: W Far . . . 6B 42
St Stephens M. ME1: Roch . . . 1C 20
St Stephen's Sq. ME15: Maid . . . 2H 43
St Werburgh Ct. ME3: Hoo W . . . 2H 11
St Werburgh Cres. ME3: Hoo W . . . 2H 11
St Werburgh Ter. ME3: Hoo W . . . 2J 11
St William's Way ME1: Roch . . . 5B 14
Salem St. ME15: Maid . . . 6K 7 (1K 43)
Salisbury Av. ME8: Gill . . . 1D 22
Salisbury Cl. ME10: Sit . . . 3G 29
Salisbury Ho. ME15: Maid . . . 5C 44
Salisbury Rd. ME4: Chat'm . . . 6E 4 (5E 14)
ME14: Maid . . . 1K 7 (5K 37)
ME20: Aylfd . . . 2B 32
Sallow Cl. ME4: St Mary . . . 6G 11
Sally Port ME7: Gill . . . 1E 4 (2E 14)
Sally Port Gdns. ME7: Gill . . . 1E 4 (2E 14)
Salmon Cres. ME12: Minst . . . 6F 53
Saltings, The ME9: Iwade . . . 2A 26
Saltings Rd. ME6: Snod . . . 3C 30
Salts Av. ME15: Loose . . . 2J 49
Salts Farm Cotts. ME15: Loose . . . 1K 49
Salts La. ME15: Loose . . . 7K 43
Saltwood Rd. ME15: Maid . . . 3J 43
Samara Cl. ME5: W'slade . . . 1E 32
Samphire Cl. ME14: Weav . . . 7D 38
Samphire Way ME4: St Mary . . . 6E 10
Samuel Dr. ME10: Kems'y . . . 5E 26
Samuels Twr. *ME5: Chat'm . . . 4F 15*
(off Longhill Av.)
Sancroft Way ME15: Maid . . . 2J 43
Sanctuary Rd. ME8: Gill . . . 5A 16
Sanctus Ct. ME3: Hoo W . . . 1J 11
Sandbourne Dr. ME14: Maid . . . 2J 37
Sanderling Way ME9: Iwade . . . 2B 26
Sanders Ct. ME12: Minst . . . 7G 53
Sandford Rd. ME10: Sit . . . 4K 25
Sandgate Ct. ME8: Parkw . . . 5F 23
Sandhill La. ME3: High'm . . . 1F 9
Sandhurst Cl. ME8: Gill . . . 5C 16
Sandlewood Ct. *ME16: Maid . . . 1D 42*
(off Tarragon Rd.)
SANDLING . . . 2J 37
Sandling Ct. ME14: Pen H . . . 4A 38
Sandling La. ME14: Maid, Pen H, S'lng . . . 1H 37
(not continuous)
Sandling Pk. ME14: Maid . . . 3J 37
Sandling Pl. Ct. ME14: Maid . . . 2J 37
Sandling Rd. ME14: Maid . . . 1H 7 (5J 37)
(Albert St.)
ME14: Maid . . . 4J 37
(Chatham Rd.)
Sandling Way ME4: St Mary . . . 6F 11
Sandown Dr. ME8: Gill . . . 2D 22
Sandown Rd. ME19: W Mal . . . 3C 34
Sandow Pl. ME19: Kings H . . . 7E 34
Sandpiper La. ME9: Iwade . . . 3C 26
Sandpiper Rd. ME5: Lord W . . . 7H 21
Sandra Ct. ME2: Strood . . . 1A 6
Sandringham Ct. ME19: Kings H . . . 3B 40
Sandringham Ho. ME1: Roch . . . 7A 6
Sandringham Rd. ME8: Parkw . . . 5E 22
Sandstone Dr. ME10: Kems'y . . . 6C 26
Sandstone Ri. ME5: W'slade . . . 2G 33
Sandycroft Rd. ME2: Strood . . . 6H 9
Sandy Dell ME7: Hpstd . . . 6A 22
Sandy La. ME6: Snod . . . 4A 30
ME14: Bear . . . 6G 39

...andy La. ME14: Boxl, Pen H ...3B 38
(not continuous)
ME19: Rya 2B 34
...andy Mt. ME14: Bear 6G 39
...anspareil Rd. ME12: Minst ...6F 53
...appers Wlk.
ME7: Gill 4H 5 (3G 15)
...apphire Cl. ME10: Sit 7A 26
...aracen A. ME4: Chat'm 7A 16
...aracen Cl. ME5: W'slade 2G 33
...arafand Gro. ME2: Strood ...4G 13
...arafand Ho. ME1: Roch 7A 6
...arsen Hgts. ME5: W'slade ...1D 32
...assoon Cl. ME20: Lark 6C 30
...atis Av. ME10: Sit 7C 26
...atis Ct. ME1: Roch 5B 6
...aunders St.
ME4: Chat'm 6B 4 (5D 14)
ME11: Maid 2G 5 (2G 15)
...avage Rd. ME5: Lord W 6F 21
...awyers Ct. ME4: Chat'm 6E 14
(not continuous)
...axon Av. ME12: Minst 6H 53
...axon Cl. ME2: Strood 6H 9
ME19: Kings H 2A 40
...axon Pl. ME2: Strood 3H 13
...axon Dr. ME14: Maid 4A 38
...axon Shore ME10: Kems'y ...5E 26
...axon Wlk. ME9: Iwade 2B 26
...axton St. ME7: Gill ...5F 5 (3G 15)
...CARBOROUGH 7G 19
...carborough Dr.
ME12: Minst 3H 53
...carborough La. ME1: Burh ..1E 30
...carlett Cl. ME5: Lord W 3G 21
...cholars Ri. ME2: Strood 1E 12
...choley Cl. ME2: Hall'g 5D 18
...chool Av. ME7: Gill ...6K 5 (4J 15)
...chool Farm Cotts.
ME1: Woul 4F 19
...chool La. ME1: Woul 4E 18
ME3: High'm 4E 4
ME9: Bap 4H 29
ME9: B'den 5H 25
ME9: Iwade 3A 26
ME9: N'tn 2D 24
ME15: Maid 3D 44
ME17: Sut V 6K 51
...chool M. ME9: Iwade 2C 26
...chool Rd. ME10: Sit 4F 29
...chool Vs. ME9: T'stall 7A 28
...chooner Wlk. ME2: Upnor ...4D 10
...chreiber M. ME7: Gill ...5K 5 (3H 15)
...cocles Rd. ME12: Minst 7H 53
...coones Cl. ME9: Bap 5J 29
...cotby Av. ME5: W'slade 5F 21
...cotchmen Cl. ME12: Minst ..5E 52
...cotney Gdns.
ME16: Maid 3G 7 (7J 37)
...cotney Ho. ME2: Strood 6A 10
...cott Av. ME8: Rain 1G 23
...cott Cl. ME20: Dit 3K 35
...cott Cl. ME4: Chat'm 6D 14
...cott's Ter.
ME4: Chat'm 7B 4 (5D 14)
...cott St. ME14: Maid ...1H 7 (5J 37)
...craces Cotts. ME16: Maid ..4D 42
...cragged Oak Caravan Pk.
ME14: Det 1G 39
...cragged Oak Rd. ME14: Det ...1G 39
...CRAPSGATE 3G 53
...crapsgate Rd. ME12: Minst ..6G 53
...crubbs La.
ME16: Maid 4F 7 (7G 37)
...eaford Ct. ME1: Roch ..6A 6 (4K 13)
...eaforth Ct. ME2: Strood ...3G 13
...eaford Ct. ME2: S'ness 2E 52
...eagull Rd. ME2: Strood 2E 12
...ealand Ct. ME1: Roch ..6A 6 (4K 13)
...ealand Dr. ME2: Strood 4G 13
...eamew Ct. ME2: Strood 1E 12
...earchlight Hgts. ME3: C'den .3E 10
...easide Av. ME12: Minst 4J 53
...eathorpe Av. ME12: Minst ...5J 53
...eaton Rd. ME7: Gill 5J 15
...eaview Rd. ME5: Gill .6H 5 (4G 15)
...eaview Ter. ME11: Queen ...7A 52
(off North Rd.)
...econd Av. ME4: Chat'm 7F 15
ME7: Gill 5J 15
ME12: S'ness 3B 52

...ecretan Rd. ME1: Roch 7K 13
...edge Cres. ME5: W'slade 5C 20
...edgemoor Ho. ME1: Roch 3C 14
...edley Cl. ME3: Cli W 2B 10
ME8: Parkw 6C 22
ME20: Aylfd 1C 36
...elbourne Rd.
ME7: Gill 1J 5 (1H 15)
...elbourne Wlk. ME15: Maid ..6E 44
...elby Rd. ME15: Maid 1E 50
...ellinge Grn. ME8: Gill 5C 16
...elsted Cl. ME8: Gill 7B 16
...elwood Cl. ME12: Maid 6E 52
...emple Gdns.
ME4: Chat'm 7A 4 (5C 14)
...enacre La. ME15: Maid 6D 44
...enacres Cotts. ME15: Maid ..6E 44
...enacre Sq. ME15: Maid 5E 44
...ENACRE WOOD 6E 44
...etford Rd. ME5: Lord W 3G 21
...ettington Av. ME5: Chat'm ..7G 15
...evern Rd. ME5: Lord W 4G 21
...evington Pk. ME15: Maid ...6J 43
...exburga Dr. ME12: Minst ...4H 53
...extant Pk.
ME2: Med E 1A 4 (2C 14)
...eymour Rd. ME5: Chat'm 5F 15
ME8: Rain 1J 23
...eymour's Cotts.
ME7: Leeds 5K 45
...hackleton Cl.
ME5: Lord W 3F 21
...hades, The ME2: Strood 1D 12
...haftesbury Cl. ME19: E Mal ..2G 35
...haftesbury Dr. ME16: Maid ..7F 37
...hakespeare Rd.
ME7: Gill 7G 5 (4G 15)
ME10: Sit 3E 28
...halder Ho. ME7: Gill ...1J 5 (1H 15)
...halfleet Cl. ME5: Chat'm ...2D 20
...hamel Bus. Cen.
ME2: Strood 1D 6 (1B 14)
...hamley Rd. ME5: Lord W 7H 21
...hanklin Cl. ME5: Chat'm ...1G 21
...harfleet Cres. ME9: Iwade ..2A 26
...harfleet Dr. ME2: Strood ...1D 12
...harnal La. ME6: Snod 3C 30
...haron Cres. ME5: W'slade ...5D 20
...harps Grn. ME7: Gill 3D 16
...harsted Way ME7: Hpstd 6A 22
ME14: Bear 6G 39
...haw Cl. ME3: Cli W 1A 10
ME14: Maid 4B 38
...hawstead Rd. ME7: Gill 2G 21
...haws Way ME1: Roch 5A 14
...haws Wood ME2: Strood 6K 9
...heals Cl. ME15: Maid ...7J 7 (2K 43)
...heal's Cres.
ME15: Maid 7J 7 (2K 43)
...hearers Cl. ME14: Weav 7D 38
...hearwater Cl. ME16: Alltn ...6E 36
...hearwater Ct. ME2: Strood ..1E 12
...hearwater Ct.
ME12: S'ness 4A 52
...HEERNESS 2C 52
...heerness Docks
ME12: S'ness 1A 52
...heerness Driving Range 4D 52
...heerness Golf Course 5F 53
...heerness Harbour Est.
ME12: S'ness 1A 52
...heerness Heritage Cen. 2C 52
(off Rose St.)
...heerness Holiday Pk.
ME12: Minst 3D 52
...heerness-on-Sea Station (Rail)
...........................2B 52
...heerness Swimming Pool, The
...........................1C 52
...heerstone Wlk. ME9: Iwade ..2B 26
...helden Dr. ME8: Rain 1F 23
(not continuous)
...heldon Bus. Cen.
ME2: Med E 7B 10
...heldon Cl. ME20: Dit 2K 35
...heldon Way ME20: Lark 7C 30
...heldrake Ho. ME7: Roch 6E 6
...helduck Cl. ME9: Iwade 3C 26
...helley Ri. ME1: Roch 5J 13
...helley Rd. ME16: Maid 2F 43
...henley Gro. ME14: S'lng ...1J 37
...hepherds Ga. ME7: Hpstd ...4K 21

...hepherds Ga. Dr.
ME14: Weav 6D 38
...hepherds Way ME17: L'ly ...1K 51
...hepperton Cl. ME5: Lord W ..5G 21
SHEPPEY COMMUNITY HOSPITAL
...........................7G 53
...heppey Ct. ME12: Minst 5D 52
...heppey Leisure Complex 1C 52
...heppey Little Theatre 2C 52
...heppey Rd. ME15: Maid 5J 43
...heppey St. ME12: S'ness ...2A 52
...heppey Way
ME9: Bob, Iwade 4J 25
(not continuous)
ME9: Iwade, Minst 1C 26
SHEPWAY 4C 44
...hepway Cl. ME15: Maid 4B 44
...heraton Cl. ME5: W'slade ...1D 32
...herbourne Dr. ME2: Strood ..6J 9
ME16: Maid 2E 42
...heridan Cl. ME5: Chat'm ...2G 21
ME14: Maid 3H 37
...heridan Ct. ME1: Roch 6J 13
...heriff Dr. ME5: W'slade 7E 20
...heringham Cl. ME16: Alltn ..4G 37
...herman Cl. ME8: Gill 7B 16
...hernolds ME15: Maid 5A 44
...herwood Av. ME5: W'slade ..6D 20
ME20: Lark 6D 30
...herwood Ho. ME5: W'slade ..6D 20
...herwoods ME5: Blue H 1B 32
...hillingheld Cl. ME14: Weav ..6E 38
...hingle Barn La.
ME15: W Far 2A 48
...hip La. ME1: Roch 4C 14
...hipley Ct.
ME14: Maid 3K 7 (7K 37)
...hipwrights Av. ME4: Chat'm .7E 14
...hirley Av. ME5: Chat'm 4B 20
...hirley Ct. ME15: Maid 7D 44
...hirley Way ME15: Bear 1F 45
...hoesmith La.
ME19: Kings H 1E 40
...holden Rd. ME2: Strood 6A 10
...hooters Chase ME9: Iwade ..2B 26
(off Stangate Dr.)
...horefields ME8: Rain 6G 17
...horeham Wlk. ME15: Maid ...5E 44
...horeway, The ME4: St Mary ..5F 11
...horland Ct.
ME1: Roch 7A 6 (4K 13)
SHORNE 4A 8
SHORNE RIDGEWAY 6A 8
...hortlands Grn. ME15: Maid ..7E 44
...hortlands Rd. ME10: Sit 3E 28
...hort St. ME4: Chat'm 5F 15
ME12: S'ness 2B 52
...horts Way ME1: Roch 5J 13
...hottenden Rd.
ME7: Gill 1J 5 (1H 15)
...hropshire Ter. ME15: Maid ..5D 44
...hrubsole Av. ME12: S'ness ..3C 52
...hrubsole Dr. ME12: S'lng ...7C 32
...hurland Av. ME10: Sit 6D 28
ME12: Minst 6H 53
...idney Rd. ME1: Roch 6J 13
ME7: Gill 1H 5 (1G 15)
...idney St. ME16: Maid 2F 43
...ienna Ct. ME8: Parkw 5C 22
...ignal Ct. ME8: Rain 7F 17
...ilchester Ct. ME14: Pen H ..4B 38
...ilverbank ME7: Chat'm 3E 20
...ilver Birches ME5: W'slade ..6E 20
...ilver Birch Wlk.
ME18: W'bury 6E 40
...ilverdale ME16: Barm 2C 42
...ilverdale Av. ME12: Minst ...6G 53
...ilverdale Dr. ME8: Gill 2F 23
...ilverdale Gro. ME10: Sit 4A 28
SILVER HILL 2K 45
...ilver Hill ME1: Roch 6H 13
ME4: Chat'm 6C 4 (5D 14)
...ilver Hill Gdns.
ME4: Chat'm 6C 4 (5D 14)
...ilverleas Certificated Site
ME15: E Far 7G 43
...ilverspot Cl. ME8: Rain 2F 23
...ilver Streak Way
ME2: Strood 4G 13
...ilver St. ME3: Wain 2K 9
...ilver Tree Cl. ME5: W'slade .1E 32
...ilverweed ME5: W'slade 7G 38

...ilverweed Rd.
ME5: W'slade 5C 20
...immonds La. ME15: Otham ...6G 45
...impson Rd. ME6: Snod 4C 30
ME10: Sit 2A 28
...inclair Cl. ME8: Parkw 4E 22
...indal Shaw Ho.
ME5: W'slade 5C 20
...indals La. ME5: Lord W 1J 33
...ingapore Dr. ME7: Gill ..2G 4 (3E 14)
(not continuous)
...ir Evelyn Rd. ME1: Roch 6K 13
...ir John Hawkins Hospital
ME1: Roch 4A 4
...ir Thomas Longley Rd.
ME2: Med E 1A 4 (1C 14)
...iskin Cl. ME1: Roch 1G 35
...issinghurst Dr. ME16: Maid ..7E 36
SITTINGBOURNE 3D 28
...ittingbourne & Kemsley
Light Railway
Kemsley Down Station ..5G 27
Milton Regis Halt Station
...........................1E 28
...ittingbourne Viaduct Station
...........................2C 28
...ittingbourne & Milton Regis
Golf Course 6D 24
...ittingbourne Community College
Sports Cen. 4G 29
...ittingbourne Heritage Mus. ..3E 28
SITTINGBOURNE
MEMORIAL HOSPITAL 4D 28
...ittingbourne Retail Pk.
ME10: Sit 2D 28
...ittingbourne Rd. ME14: Det ..3D 38
(not continuous)
ME14: Maid 6A 38
(not continuous)
...ittingbourne Road (Maidstone)
(Park & Ride) 4C 38
...ittingbourne Viaduct Station
...ittingbourne & Kemsley
Light Railway 2C 28
...ittingbourne Station (Rail) ...3D 28
...ix Poor Travellers House
...........................4C 6 (2A 14)
...keleton Hill ME1: Woul 5F 19
...kene Cl. ME8: Rain 7G 17
...kinners Cl. ME20: Eccl 4J 31
...kinner St.
ME4: Chat'm 6C 4 (5D 14)
ME7: Gill 4G 5 (3G 15)
(not continuous)
...kinners Way ME17: L'ly 1K 51
...kua Ct. ME2: Strood 1E 12
...kye Cl. ME15: Maid 5K 43
...lade Cl. ME5: Lord W 7F 21
...latin Rd. ME2: Strood 7K 9
...licketts Hill
ME4: Chat'm 5D 4 (4E 14)
...lipway Rd. ME7: Gill 1A 52
...mall Hythe Cl. ME15: Bear ..2G 45
...mall Profits ME18: Yald 7G 41
...marden Wlk. ME8: Rain 7H 17
...marts Cotts. ME14: Bear ...7H 39
(off The Green)
...meed Cl. ME10: Sit 3F 29
...meed Dean Cen. ME10: Sit ..3E 28
...metham Gdns. ME2: Strood ..6K 9
...mith Rd. ME5: Lord W 6F 21
...miths Est. ME4: S'lng 7C 32
...mith's Hill ME15: W Far 7K 41
...mith St. ME2: Strood 2J 13
...nipe Ct. ME2: Strood 1E 12
SNIPESHILL 4G 29
...nodhurst Av. ME5: Chat'm ...4C 20
...nodhurst Ho. ME5: Chat'm ..2E 20
SNODLAND 2C 30
...nodland By-Pass
ME6: Hall'g, Snod 5B 30
...nodland Millennium Mus. ...2C 30
...nodland Rd. ME6: Snod 3A 30
ME19: Birl, Snod 3A 30
...nodland Station (Rail) 2D 30
...nowdon Av. ME14: Maid 6A 38
...nowdon Cl. ME5: Chat'm 2F 21
...nowdon Pde. ME14: Maid ...6B 38
...nowdrop Wlk. ME10: Sit 6D 28
...olent Gdns. ME5: Chat'm ...2F 21
...olent Ho. ME2: Strood 3G 13
...oll Leisure
Chatham 2D 20

Solomon Rd.—Swallows Leisure Centre, The

Solomon Rd. ME8: Rain 7F 17
Solomons Rd.
ME4: Chat'm 4C 4 (4D 14)
SOMERFIELD BMI HOSPITAL . . .6G 37
Somerfield Cl. ME16: Maid 7G 37
Somerfield La. ME16: Maid 6G 37
Somerfield Rd. ME16: Maid 7G 37
Somerset Cl. ME5: Chat'm 1G 21
ME10: Sit 3A 28
Somerset Rd. ME15: Maid 4B 44
Somner Wlk. ME15: Maid 1E 50
Sonora Av. ME10: Sit 1A 28
Sonora Way ME10: Sit 1A 28
Sorrel Cl. ME12: Minst 7H 53
Sorrell Rd. ME5: W'slade 5D 20
Sortmill Rd. ME6: Snod 3D 30
South Av. ME8: Gill 6A 16
ME10: Sit 4E 28
Sth. Aylesford Retail Pk.
ME20: Aylfd 3B 36
South Bank ME17: Sut V 6K 51
Southbourne Gro.
ME5: W'slade 5E 20
Sth. Bush La. ME8: Rain 3H 23
South Cres. ME17: Cox 2F 49
Southdown Rd. ME12: Minst 6E 52
Sth. Eastern Rd.
ME2: Strood 1B 6 (1A 14)
Southey Way ME20: Lark 6B 30
Southfields ME1: Roch 5K 13
Southill Rd.
ME4: Chat'm 7B 4 (5D 14)
South La. ME17: Sut V 7K 51
South Pk. Bus. Village
ME15: Maid 3K 43
South Pk. Rd. ME15: Maid 3A 44
Sth. Pondside Rd.
ME4: Chat'm 7E 10
South Rd. ME4: Chat'm 1E 14
(Gordon Rd.)
ME4: Chat'm 7F 11
(Officer's Rd.)
Southsea Av. ME12: Minst 3H 53
South Shore *ME7: Gill 1H 15*
(off Ocean Dr.)
Sth. Side Three Rd.
ME4: Chat'm 7F 11
South St. ME11: Queen 7A 52
ME16: Barm 3B 42
South Vw. ME14: Bear 7H 39
Southview Gdns.
ME12: S'ness 4C 52
Southwark Rd. ME2: Strood 2F 13
South Ways ME17: Sut V 6J 51
Southwell Rd. ME2: Strood 2E 12
Southwood ME16: Barm 2C 42
South Wood Local Nature Reserve
. . . . .4K 21
Sovereign Blvd. ME7: Gill 6J 15
Sovereign Ct. ME2: Strood 1E 12
Sovereigns, The ME16: Maid . . .7G 37
Space Bus. Cen.
ME2: Strood 2J 13
Spade La. ME9: H'lip 4J 23
Spearhead Rd. ME14: Maid 4J 37
Spectrum Bus. Cen.
ME2: Med E 7C 10
Spectrum Bus. Est.
ME15: Maid 1E 50
Spectrum W. ME16: Alltn 3G 37
Speedwell Av. ME5: W'slade 5C 20
Speedwell Cl. ME7: Gill 3J 15
ME14: Weav 7D 38
Spekes Rd. ME7: Hpstd 3B 22
Speldhurst Ct. ME16: Maid 7G 37
Spembly Ct. ME4: Chat'm 4A 4
Spencer Cl. ME5: W'slade 4E 20
Spencer Flats ME5: Chat'm 1F 21
Spencer Pl.
ME19: Kings H 1C 40
Spencer Way ME15: Maid 5D 44
Spenlow Dr. ME5: W'slade 1E 32
Sperrin Pl. ME2: Strood 3G 13
Spicer Homes ME10: Sit 5D 28
Spiers, The ME7: Gill 3C 16
Spillway, The ME15: Maid 2G 43
Spindle Glade ME14: Maid 6B 38
Spindlewood Cl.
ME5: Lord W 6F 21
Spinel Cl. ME10: Sit 1A 28
Spinnaker Ct. ME1: Roch 7A 14
Spinney, The ME5: W'slade 1E 32
ME15: Maid 2A 44
Spires, The ME2: Strood 3F 13
ME16: Maid 7G 37
Spitfire Cl. ME5: Lord W 3F 21
Spitfire Rd. ME19: Kings H 1A 40
Splashes Leisure Cen. 7D 16
Sportsfield ME14: Maid 6A 38
Sportsmans Cotts.
ME19: Kings H 6C 34
Spot Farm Cotts.
ME15: Otham 5J 45
Spot La. ME15: Bear 2E 44
Sprig, The ME14: Bear 7F 39
Spring Cotts. ME17: Lint 7G 49
Springett Cl. ME20: Eccl 4H 31
SPRINGETTS HILL 4E 34
Springett Way ME17: Cox 1G 49
SPRINGFIELD 5J 37
Springfield Av. ME14: Maid 4J 37
Springfield Rd.
ME7: Gill 3K 5 (2J 15)
ME10: Sit 2B 28
ME20: Lark 6B 30
Springfield Ter.
ME4: Chat'm 5B 4 (4D 14)
Spring Gdn. Pas.
ME12: S'ness 2C 52
(off High St.)
Springvale ME8: Wigm 3C 22
ME9: Iwade 2B 26
ME16: Maid 4F 7 (7H 37)
Springwood Cl. ME16: Barm 1D 42
Springwood Rd. ME16: Barm . . .1D 42
Sprotshill Cl. ME10: Sit 1C 28
Spruce Cl. ME20: Lark 1H 35
Spurgeon's Cotts.
ME17: Lint 3H 49
Spurway ME14: Bear 7F 39
Sqaure Hill ME15: Maid 7A 38
Square, The ME10: Kems'y 5D 26
ME15: Hunt 6A 48
Square Hill Rd. ME15: Maid 1A 44
Squires Cl. ME2: Strood 1D 12
Stable Cl. ME5: Lord W 4G 21
Stable Cotts. ME15: E Far 5F 43
Staceys St.
ME14: Maid 1H 7 (6J 37)
Stadium Bus. Pk. ME10: Sit 1F 29
Stadium Way ME10: Sit 1G 29
Stadler Cl. ME16: Alltn 4G 37
Staffa Rd. ME15: Maid 5K 43
Stafford Gdns.
ME15: Maid 7G 7 (2J 43)
Stafford St. ME7: Gill 5F 5 (3F 15)
Stag Rd. ME5: Lord W 4F 21
Stagshaw Cl.
ME15: Maid 7J 7 (2K 43)
Stake La. ME2: Hall'g 3C 18
Stalham Ct. ME7: Hpstd 5B 22
Stalin Av. ME5: Chat'm 1F 21
Stampers, The ME15: Maid 2G 43
Standen Cl. ME8: Parkw 5E 22
Standen Gro. ME10: Sit 2G 29
Stanford Dr. ME16: Maid 1F 43
Stanford Way ME2: Cux 6E 12
Stangate Dr. ME9: Iwade 2B 26
Stangate Rd. ME2: Strood 1E 12
Stanhope Av. ME10: Sit 4D 28
Stanhope Cl. ME14: Maid 4H 37
Stanhope Ho. ME15: Maid 3H 43
Stanhope Rd. ME2: Strood 1J 13
Stanley Av. ME11: Queen 7A 52
ME12: Minst 5K 53
Stanley Ct. ME7: Gill 2K 15
Stanley Rd. ME5: Lord W 3G 21
ME7: Gill 2H 5 (2G 15)
Stansted Cl. ME16: Alltn 4F 37
Staple Cl. ME10: Sit 2C 28
Staplehurst Lodge Ind. Est.
ME10: Sit 2A 28
Staplehurst Rd. ME8: Gill 5B 16
ME10: Sit 2A 28
(Bourne Gro.)
ME10: Sit 3K 25
(Conqueror Ct.)
Staplers Ct. ME14: Pen H 3A 38
Star Ct. ME15: Loose 2J 49
Star Hill ME1: Roch 6D 6 (3B 14)
Star La. ME7: Gill 1K 21
Star Mill Ct. ME5: Chat'm 6H 15
Star Mill La. ME5: Chat'm 6H 15
Starnes Ct.
ME14: Maid 2J 7 (6K 37)
Starveacre La. ME9: B'den 7K 25
Station App. ME2: Hall'g 4C 18
ME16: Maid 5G 7 (1J 43)
ME19: W Mal 3E 34
Station Hill ME15: E Far 5D 42
Station Hill Cotts.
ME15: E Far 5D 42
Station Rd. ME2: Cux 6E 12
ME2: Strood 2A 6 (7K 9)
ME8: Rain 7F 17
ME9: N'tn 3D 24
ME14: Maid 2H 7 (6J 37)
(not continuous)
ME17: H'shm 6K 47
ME20: Dit, Aylfd 2K 35
Station Rd. Nth. ME19: W Mal . . .3E 34
Station St. ME10: Sit 3C 28
Station Vw. Ct. *ME10: Sit 3C 28*
(off Pembury St.)
Steadman Cl. ME3: High'm 1E 8
Steele St. ME2: Strood 7J 9
Steerforth Cl. ME1: Roch 6A 14
Step Style ME10: Sit 5F 29
Sterling Av. ME16: Alltn 6F 37
Sterling Rd. ME10: Sit 6B 28
ME11: Queen 7A 52
Sterry Gdns. ME15: Maid 5D 44
Steven Cl.
ME4: Chat'm 7E 4 (5E 14)
Stevens Cl. ME6: Snod 2C 30
Stevenson Cl.
ME15: Maid 6H 7 (1J 43)
Stevenson Way ME20: Lark 6B 30
Stevens Rd. ME20: Eccl 4H 31
Stewart Ho. ME3: C'den 1C 10
Stickens La. ME19: E Mal 5F 35
Stickfast La.
ME9: Bob . . . . .1K 25 & 6A 26
Stilebridge La.
ME17: Bou Mo 7K 49
Stiles Cl. ME12: Minst 6G 53
Stillwater M. ME4: St Mary 5F 11
Stirling Cen.
Rochester 2A 20
Stirling Cl. ME1: Roch 5J 13
ME8: Parkw 5E 22
Stirling Pk. ME1: Roch 3A 20
Stirling Rd. ME19: Kings H 1A 40
Stockbury Dr. ME16: Alltn 4G 37
Stock Cl. ME1: Roch 7A 14
Stockers Brow ME9: Rod 7E 28
Stockers Hill ME9: Rod 7E 28
Stockett La.
ME15: E Far, Maid 3H 43
ME17: Cox 2F 49
Stockton Cl. ME14: Pen H 3A 38
Stoke Rd. ME3: Hoo W 2J 11
Stoneacre 5G 45
Stoneacre Cl. ME8: Parkw 4D 22
Stoneacre Cotts.
ME15: Otham 5H 45
Stoneacre Ct. ME15: Maid 3K 43
Stoneacre La. ME15: Otham 4G 45
Stone Cotts. ME15: E Far 5C 42
ME15: Maid 3C 44
ME17: L'ly 1G 51
Stonecrop Cl. ME4: St Mary 6G 11
Stonecross Lea
ME5: Chat'm 7G 15
Stonehorse Ct. ME3: Strood 4J 9
Stonehorse La. ME2: Strood 4J 9
ME3: Strood 4J 9
Stones Fishery 4D 52
Stoney Bank ME7: Gill 1K 21
Stoney Hill ME5: Chat'm 5F 15
Stony La. ME1: Roch 3K 19
Stopford Rd.
ME7: Gill 7H 5 (4G 15)
Storway Ct. ME2: Strood 3J 13
Stour Cl. ME2: Strood 1H 13
Strachan Cl. ME15: Maid 3K 43
STRAND, THE 1J 15
Strand App. Rd. ME7: Gill 1J 15
Strand Leisure Pool & Park 1J 15
Strand Roundabout, The
ME7: Gill 1J 15
Stratford Av. ME8: Gill 1D 22
Stratford Dr. ME15: Maid 6C 44
Stratford La. ME8: Rain 1F 23
Stratford Rd. ME19: W Mal 3B 34
Straw Mill Hill ME15: Maid 3H 43
Stream, The ME20: Dit 2K 35
Stream Cotts. ME14: S'lng 2H 37
Streamside ME20: Dit 2J 35
Street, The DA12: Shorne 4A
ME2: Hall'g 5A 1
ME7: B'hst 7B 2
ME9: Bap 4H 2
ME9: B'den 7J 2
ME9: H'lip 5K 2
ME9: Iwade 2C 2
ME14: Bear 7H 3
ME14: Boxl 1B 3
ME14: Det 2F 3
ME18: Tstn 5H 4
Street End Rd. ME5: Chat'm 1F 2
Street Farm Cotts.
ME3: Hoo W 1K 1
Streetfield Rd. ME8: Rain 7F 1
Strode Cres. ME12: S'ness 2C 5
STROOD 1A 6 (1K 13
Strood Leisure Cen. 1H 1
Strood Retail Pk.
ME2: Strood 2A 6 (1K 13
Strood Station (Rail) 1B 6 (1A 14
Strood Yacht Club 2J 1
Strover St. ME7: Gill 1G 5 (1G 15
Stuart Cl. ME14: Maid 5A 3
Stuart Rd. ME7: Gill 5H 1
Sturdee Av. ME7: Gill 6K 5 (4J 15
Sturdee Cotts. ME3: Hoo W 1K 1
Sturla Rd.
ME4: Chat'm 7D 4 (6E 14
Sturmer Ct. ME19: Kings H 2B 4
Sturry Way ME8: Gill 6C 1
Style Cl. ME8: Parkw 5E 2
Styles Cl. ME10: Sit 2G 2
Styles La. ME14: Boxl 7G 3
Suffolk Av. ME8: Rain 7F 1
Suffolk Ct. ME8: Rain 7F 1
Suffolk Rd. ME15: Maid 4C 4
Sugarloaf Hill ME5: Chat'm 6H 1
Sultan Rd. ME5: Lord W 1G 3
Summer Ct. ME14: Maid 1K
Summerson Cl. ME1: Roch 7A 1
Summerville Av.
ME12: Minst 7F 5
Sunderland Cl. ME1: Roch 5J 1
Sunderland Dr. ME8: Rain 1G 2
Sunderland Ho. ME7: Gill 1G
Sunderland Quay
ME2: Med E 3E 6 (2B 14
Sundridge Dr. ME5: W'slade 5E 2
Sundridge Hill
ME2: Cux, Strood 6E 1
Sungold Wlk. ME19: Kings H . . .1C 4
Sunningdale Cl. ME8: Gill 3D 2
Sunningdale Ct. ME15: Maid 7A 3
Sunningdale Dr. ME8: Gill 3D 2
Sunny Bank ME10: Sit 2F 2
Sunnyfields Cl. ME8: Gill 1E 2
Sunnyfields Dr. ME12: Minst 6C 52
Sunnymead Av. ME7: Gill 3J 1
Sunnyside Av. ME12: Minst 6G 53
Sun Pier ME4: Chat'm 3A 4 (3C 14,
Sunrise Way ME19: Kings H 1D 4
Sunstone Dr. ME10: Sit 7A 2
Sun Ter. ME5: W'slade 5F 2
Superabbey Est. ME20: Aylfd 1F 3
Surrey Rd. ME15: Maid 4C 4
Sussex Dr. ME5: W'slade 5E 2
Sussex Rd. ME15: Maid 3C 4
Sutherland Gdns. ME8: Gill 3E 2
Sutton Cl. ME8: Rain 1G 23
Sutton Hgts.
ME15: Maid 6D 44
Sutton Rd. ME15: Maid 4A 44
ME17: L'ly, Sut V 1H 51
Sutton St. ME14: Bear 1J 45
SUTTON VALENCE 6K 51
Sutton Valence Hill
ME17: Sut V 6K 51
Swain Cl. ME2: Strood 7H 9
Swain Rd. ME8: Wigm 3B 22
Swale Av. ME12: S'ness 3B 52
Swale Ho. ME10: Sit 3E 28
Swale Indoor Bowls Cen. 1B 28
Swale Rd. ME2: Strood 1E 12
Swale Way
ME10: Iwade, Kems'y 4D 26
ME10: Sit 7G 27
Swallow Av. ME9: Iwade 2C 26
Swallow Ho. ME16: Maid 4F 7
Swallow Ri. ME5: W'slade 4E 20
Swallow Rd. ME20: Lark 1G 35
Swallows Leisure Centre, The
. . . . .4D 28

Union Pk.—Wellington Rd.

Union Pk. ME15: Maid 1E 50
Union Pl. ME4: Chat'm . . .5D 4 (4E 14)
Union Rd. ME12: Minst 5J 53
Union St. ME1: Roch 6C 6 (3A 14)
ME4: Chat'm 5D 4 (4E 14)
ME12: S'ness 2A 52
ME14: Maid 3J 7 (7K 37)
Unity Ct. ME12: S'ness 2D 52
Unity St. ME10: Sit 4C 28
ME12: S'ness 2D 52
University of Greenwich
Medway Campus 7F 11
Sports Hall 7F 11
University of Kent
Medway Campus 7F 11
(off Pembroke)
Unwin Cl. ME20: Aylfd 7J 31
Upbury Way
ME4: Chat'm 5E 4 (4E 14)
Upchat Rd. ME2: Upnor 3C 10
ME3: C'den, Upnor 3C 10
UPCHURCH 5K 17
Upchurch River Valley Golf Course
. . . . .6K 17
Uplands Cl. ME2: Strood 2F 13
Uplands Way ME12: Minst 7C 52
Upnor Castle 5D 10
Upnor Rd.
ME2: Strood, Upnor 6B 10
Upnor Sailing Club 4E 10
Up. Barn Hill ME15: Hunt 2B 48
Up. Britton Pl.
ME7: Gill 5F 5 (3F 15)
UPPER BUSH 6B 12
Up. Bush Rd. ME2: Cux 6B 12
Up. Chimes ME14: Bear 6F 39
Up. East Rd. ME4: Chat'm 7F 11
Up. Fans La. ME9: Iwade 2A 26
Up. Fant Rd. ME16: Maid 2F 43
Upper Fld. Rd. ME10: Sit 2F 29
UPPER HALLING 4A 18
Up. Hunton Hill ME15: E Far 2D 48
Up. Luton Rd. ME5: Chat'm 5G 15
Upper Mill ME18: W'bury 4E 40
ME19: E Mal 4G 35
Upper Rd. ME15: Maid . . .7K 7 (2A 44)
Up. Stone St.
ME15: Maid 5K 7 (1K 43)
Upper St. ME17: Holl 1F 47
ME17: Leeds 7A 46
UPPER UPNOR 5D 10
Urquhart Cl. ME5: W'slade 4E 20
Utah Ri. ME3: Wain 4B 10

V

Vale Dr. ME5: Chat'm 4B 20
Valence Ho. ME15: Maid 5B 44
Valenciennes Ho.
ME4: Chat'm 5E 4
Valenciennes Rd. ME10: Sit 4C 28
Valentine Cl. ME8: Gill 7A 16
Valentine Rd. ME15: Maid 5D 44
Valerian Cl. ME5: W'slade 5C 20
Vale Rd. ME15: Loose 1H 49
Valetta Way
ME1: Roch 7A 6 (4K 13)
Valiant Rd. ME5: Lord W 7G 21
Valley, The ME17: Cox 2G 49
Valley Dr. ME15: Maid 7J 43
Valley Ri. ME5: W'slade 7D 20
Valley Rd. ME7: Gill 4J 15
Valley Vw. Rd. ME1: Roch 6K 13
Vancouver Dr. ME8: Gill 7C 16
Vange Cott. M.
ME1: Roch 7A 6 (4K 13)
Vanguard Way
ME2: Med E, Upnor 7C 10
Vanity La. ME17: Lint 4G 49
Varnes St. ME20: Eccl 4H 31
Vaughan Dr. ME10: Kems'y 6D 26
Vauxhall Cres.
ME6: Snod 4B 30
Vectis Dr. ME10: Sit 6D 26
Veles Rd. ME6: Snod 2B 30
Velum Dr. ME10: Sit 1A 28
Ventnor Cl. ME5: Chat'm 1G 21
Vicarage Cl. ME2: Hall'g 4C 18
ME20: Aylfd 7H 31
Vicarage Ct. ME9: N'tn 2D 24
Vicarage La. ME3: Hoo W 2J 11
ME15: E Far 5D 42
Vicarage Rd. ME2: Hall'g 4A 18
ME2: Strood 1A 6 (7K 9)
ME7: Gill 5G 5 (3G 15)
ME10: Sit 1B 28
ME12: Minst 5K 53
Vicarage Row ME3: High'm 3E 8
Vicary Way ME16: Maid 6G 37
Victoria Ct. ME15: E Far 1C 48
ME16: Maid 5F 7 (1H 43)
Victoria Dr. ME19: Kings H 3A 40
Victoria M. ME10: Sit 3E 28
Victoria Orchard ME16: Maid 1E 42
Victoria Pde.
ME14: Maid 2H 7 (6J 37)
Victoria Rd. ME4: Chat'm 6F 15
ME5: W'slade 7C 20
ME10: Sit 3B 28
Victoria St. ME1: Roch . . .6C 6 (3B 14)
ME2: Strood 1A 6 (1K 13)
ME7: Gill 4H 5 (3G 15)
ME12: S'ness 3B 52
ME16: Maid 5F 7 (1H 43)
ME20: Eccl 4H 31
Victoria Ter. ME1: Roch 6J 13
ME10: Sit 3B 28
Victory Ct. ME7: Gill 5J 5
Victory Dr. ME19: Kings H 1E 40
Victory Mnr. *ME7: Gill 2E 14*
(off Middle St.)
Victory Pk. ME2: Med E 1C 14
Victory St. ME12: S'ness 2B 52
Vidal Mnr. ME7: Gill 4G 5
Vidgeon Av. ME3: Hoo W 1G 11
Viewlands ME5: Chat'm 5G 15
Viewpoint ME14: Pen H 3B 38
View Rd. ME3: Cli W 2A 10
Vigor Cl. ME19: E Mal 4G 35
Viking Cl. ME2: Strood 4H 13
Village Hotel Leisure Club 2H 37
Village Vw. ME5: Chat'm 6G 15
Villa Rd. ME3: High'm 4D 8
Vincent Ct. ME12: S'ness 3C 52
Vincent Gdns. ME12: S'ness 3C 52
Vincent Rd. ME10: Sit 4G 29
ME20: Aylfd 3A 32
Vine Ct. ME18: W'bury 4F 41
Vine M. ME16: Maid 5F 7
Vineries, The ME7: Gill 3J 15
Viners Cl. ME10: Sit 6C 28
Vines La. ME1: Roch 5B 6 (3A 14)
Vineyard Cres. ME8: Rain 7H 17
Vineyard M. ME8: Rain 7H 17
Viney Cotts. ME17: Leeds 6A 46
VINTERS PARK 6B 38
Vinters Pk. 6C 38
Vinters Pk. Crematorium
ME14: Weav 5C 38
Vinters Rd. ME14: Maid 6A 38
Vinters Valley Nature Reserve
. . . . .6C 38
Vintners Ct. ME14: Weav 7D 38
Vintners Way ME14: Weav 7D 38
Violet Cl. ME5: W'slade 2E 32
ME12: Minst 7H 53
Violet Ct. ME10: Sit 5D 28
Virgin Active
Rochester 4H 13
Virginia Ct. ME4: Chat'm 7A 4
Virginia Rd. ME7: Gill 1H 5 (1G 15)
Vixen Cl. ME5: Lord W 3G 21
Volante Dr. ME10: Sit 7C 26
Vulcan Cl. ME5: Chat'm 2F 21

W

Wadham Pl. ME10: Sit 5F 29
Waghorn Rd. ME6: Snod 2C 30
Waghorn St. ME4: Chat'm 5F 15
Wagoners Cl.
ME14: Weav 7D 38
Wain Ct. ME12: Minst 7G 53
WAINSCOTT 5B 10
Wainscott Rd. ME2: Wain 5B 10
Wainscott Wlk. ME2: Wain 4B 10
Wakefield Cl. ME2: Strood 2F 13
Wakehurst Cl. ME17: Cox 2E 48
Wakeley Rd. ME8: Rain 7G 17
Wake Rd. ME1: Roch 1A 20
WALDERSLADE 6E 20
WALDERSLADE BOTTOM 6E 20
Walderslade Cen.
ME5: W'slade 6E 20
Walderslade Rd.
ME4: Chat'm 1D 20
ME5: Chat'm, W'slade 3D 20
(not continuous)
Walderslade Village By-Pass
ME5: W'slade 6D 20
Walderslade Woods
ME5: W'slade 6B 20
Waldron Dr. ME15: Maid 6J 43
Wall, The ME10: Sit 2C 28
Wallace Rd. ME1: Roch 1C 20
Wallbridge La. ME8: Rain 5J 17
Wall Cl. ME3: Hoo W 1H 11
Wallers Cotts. ME15: E Far 1C 48
Walleys Cl. ME8: Rain 7H 17
Wallis Av. ME15: Maid 7D 44
Wallis Oak Av. ME15: Maid 7E 44
Wallis Pl. ME16: Maid . . .6G 7 (1J 43)
Walmer Ct.
ME14: Maid 2K 7 (6K 37)
Walmer Gdns. ME10: Sit 2B 28
Walmer Ho. *ME2: Strood 6A 10*
(off Cypress Ct.)
Walmers Av. ME3: High'm 3C 8
Walnut Cl. ME5: Chat'm 1F 21
Walnut Row ME20: Dit 3J 35
Walnut Tree Av. ME15: Maid 7K 43
Walnut Tree Cotts.
ME15: Maid 7K 43
Walnut Tree Ct. ME20: Lark 2J 35
Walnut Tree Dr. ME10: Sit 3B 28
Walnut Tree La. ME15: Maid 7K 43
Walpole Cl. ME19: E Mal 2G 35
Walsby Dr. ME10: Kems'y 6E 26
Walsham Rd. ME5: W'slade 1D 32
Walshaw Ho.
ME14: Maid 1J 7 (5K 37)
Walsingham Cl. ME8: Parkw 6D 22
Walsingham Ho.
ME14: Maid 1K 7 (5K 37)
Walter Burke Av. ME1: Woul 4E 18
Walter Burke Way
ME4: Chat'm 7E 10
Walters Rd. ME3: Hoo W 1J 11
Waltham Rd. ME8: Gill 5B 16
Warbler's Cl. ME2: Strood 1J 13
Warden Cl. ME16: Maid 7F 37
Warden Mill Cl.
ME18: W'bury 5E 40
Warden Rd. ME1: Roch 6A 14
Warden Ter. *ME18: W'bury 6E 40*
(off Maidstone Rd.)
Warde's Cotts. ME15: Otham . . .4G 45
Wards Hill Rd. ME12: Minst 4H 53
Ward Vw. ME5: Chat'm 6H 15
Wardwell La.
ME9: Lwr Hal, N'tn 2E 24
WARE STREET 6F 39
Ware St. ME14: Weav, Bear 6E 38
Warlingham Cl. ME8: Rain 7G 17
WARMLAKE 4K 51
Warmlake ME17: Sut V 4K 51
Warmlake Bus. Est.
ME17: Sut V 4K 51
Warmlake Rd.
ME17: Cha S, Sut V 4G 51
Warner St.
ME4: Chat'm 7C 4 (5D 14)
Warnett Ct. ME6: Snod 1C 30
Warnford Gdns. ME15: Maid 4K 43
Warren Cl. ME10: Sit 5F 29
Warren La. ME9: H'lip 6J 23
Warren Rd.
DA13: Cux, Lud'n 5A 12
ME5: Blue H 2B 32
Warren Vw. DA12: Shorne 4A 8
Warren Wood Rd. ME1: Roch . . .2A 20
Warwick Cres. ME1: Roch 6H 13
ME10: Sit 2A 28
Warwick Pl. ME16: Maid 1H 43
Washington Ho. ME15: Maid 7D 44
Watchmans Ter. ME5: Chat'm . . .6H 15
Waterfront Leisure Cen.
Gillingham 7J 11
Waterfront Way
ME4: Chat'm 4B 4 (4D 14)
WATERINGBURY 4F 41
Wateringbury Rd.
ME19: E Mal 1G 41
Wateringbury Station (Rail) 6F 41
Water La. ME14: Bear, T'hm 7J 39
ME15: Hunt 7A 48
ME15: Maid 4J 7
Water La. ME17: H'shm 6H 4
ME19: W Mal 3D 3
Waterloo Hill ME12: Minst 6J 5
Waterloo Rd.
ME7: Gill 6G 5 (4G 1
ME10: Sit 2B 2
Waterloo St.
ME15: Maid 6K 7 (1K 4
Waterlow Rd.
ME14: Maid 1K 7 (5K 3
Water Mdw. Cl.
ME7: Hpstd 3K 2
Watermill Cl. ME2: Strood 7A 1
ME16: Alltn 6E 3
Watermill M. ME10: Sit 2C 2
Waters Edge
ME15: Maid 7G 7 (2J 4
Waterside Ct. ME2: Med E 2D 1
ME4: Chat'm 7E 1
ME19: Leyb 7A 3
Waterside Ga.
ME16: Alltn 2G 7 (6J 37
Waterside La. ME7: Gill 1K 1
Waterside M.
ME18: W'bury 6E 4
Waterside Quay ME20: Aylfd 1E 3
Watersmeet ME4: St Mary 6F 1
Watersmeet Cl. ME15: Maid 3K 4
Waters Pl. ME7: Hpstd 3A 2
Waterview Bus. Cen.
ME10: Sit 7G 2
Waterway, The ME9: Iwade 2B 2
Water Works Cotts.
ME1: Roch 1J 1
Waterworks Cotts.
ME14: Boxl 6G 3
ME14: Weav 4E 3
Watling Av. ME5: Chat'm 6H 1
Watling Pl. ME10: Sit 4E 2
Watling St. ME2: Strood 7E
ME5: Chat'm, Gill 6H 1
ME7: Gill 6H 1
ME8: Gill 6A 1
Watson Av. ME5: Chat'm 4B 2
Watsons Hill ME10: Sit 2C 2
Watts Almshouses
ME1: Roch 7B 6 (4A 14
Watts Av. ME1: Roch 7B 6 (4A 14
Watts Cl. ME6: Snod 2D 3
Watts' St.
ME4: Chat'm 6A 4 (5C 14
Wat Tyler Way
ME15: Maid 5K 7 (7K 37
Waverley Av. ME12: Minst 5H 5
Waverley Cl. ME5: Lord W 7H 2
ME17: Cox 3F 4
WAYFIELD 2E 2
Wayfield Rd. ME5: Chat'm 2D 2
Waylands ME14: Bear 7G 3
Wayne Ct. ME2: Wain 5B 1
Weald Cl. ME15: Maid 6B 4
Weald Ct. ME10: Sit 5B 2
Wealden Ct. ME5: Chat'm 5F 1
Wealden Way ME20: Aylfd 4B 3
Weatherly Cl. ME1: Roch 7C
Weavering Cl. ME2: Strood 5K
Weavering Cotts.
ME14: Weav 1D 4
WEAVERING STREET 6E 3
Weavering St. ME14: Weav 7D 3
Weavers, The ME16: Alltn 7E 3
Weavers Ct. ME1: Roch 6C
Webb Cl. ME3: Hoo W 1H 1
Webster Rd. ME8: Rain 7F 1
Wedgewood Cl. ME16: Alltn 6E 3
Wedgewood Dr.
ME5: Chat'm 2E 2
WEEDS WOOD 5D 2
Weeds Wood Rd.
ME5: W'slade 5D 2
Weekes Ct. *ME11: Queen 7A 5*
(off Mount Fld.
Week St. ME14: Maid 2H 7 (6K 37
Weir Mill ME19: E Mal 4G 3
Welcombe Ct. *ME8: Gill 1D 2*
(off Derwent Way
Well Cotts. ME14: Det 2F 3
Weller Av. ME1: Roch 6B 1
Wellesley Rd. ME12: S'ness 2D 5
Wellington Pl. ME14: Maid 5J 3
Wellington Rd.
ME7: Gill 7H 5 (4G 15
ME10: Sit 4K 2

78 A-Z Maidstone & Medway Towns

Wellington Way—Woodford Rd.

Wellington Way
ME19: Kings H 1A **40**
Wellmarsh ME12: S'ness 2A **52**
Well Rd. ME11: Queen 7A **52**
ME14: Maid 1J **7** (6K **37**)
Wells Ct. ME2: Strood 3F **13**
Wells Ho. ME10: Sit 3F **29**
ME15: Maid 5C **44**
Wells Rd. ME2: Strood 3F **13**
WELL STREET 5F **35**
Well St. ME15: Loose 1H **49**
ME19: E Mal 5E **34**
Wellwinch Rd. ME10: Sit 2B **28**
Wemmick Cl. ME1: Roch 2B **20**
Wendover Cl. ME2: Hall'g 4D **18**
Wents, The ME15: E Far 2D **48**
Wents Wood ME14: Weav 6E **38**
Wentworth Ct. ME10: Sit 2F **29**
Wentworth Dr. ME3: Cli W 1A **10**
ME8: Gill 2E **22**
ME10: Sit 2A **28**
Wentworth Ho. ME10: Sit 2A **28**
Wesley Cl. ME16: Barm 1C **42**
Westborough M.
ME16: Maid 1E **42**
Westbourne Ho. *ME2: Strood 4G 13*
(off Whitehead Dr.)
Westbourne St. ME10: Sit 3C **28**
Westbrooke Cl. ME4: Chat'm 6E **14**
Westcliff Dr. ME12: Minst 4K **53**
West Ct. ME15: Maid 3K **43**
Westcourt St. ME7: Gill 2E **14**
West Dr. ME5: Chat'm 4B **20**
Westergate Rd.
ME2: Strood 6H **9**
Westerham Cl. ME8: Gill 4B **16**
Westerham Rd. ME10: Sit 4A **28**
Westerhill Rd.
ME17: Lint, Cox 4F **49**
Western Av. ME4: Chat'm 7E **10**
ME12: Minst 6D **52**
Western Rd. ME16: Maid 2F **43**
WEST FARLEIGH 6A **42**
Westfield Bus. Cen.
ME2: Strood 1B **6** (1A **14**)
Westfield Gdns. ME9: B'den 6E **24**
WESTFIELD SOLE 3G **33**
Westfield Sole Rd.
ME14: Boxl 2G **33**
Westfield Wood Nature Reserve
4D **32**
Westgate ME4: St Mary 5F **11**
West Grn. ME10: Kems'y 5D **26**
Westlands Av. ME10: Sit 5K **25**
West La. ME10: Sit 3E **28**
(Smeed Dean Cen.)
ME10: Sit 3E **28**
(The Turrets)
ME12: S'ness 2A **52**
West La. Trad. Est.
ME10: Sit 2E **28**
WEST MALLING 3D **34**
W. Malling Air Station
ME19: Kings H 7B **34**
W. Malling By-Pass
ME19: W Mal 5D **34**
W. Malling Ind. Pk.
ME19: Addtn 1A **34**
West Malling Station (Rail) 3E **34**
W. Marsh Cl. ME15: Maid 5E **44**
Westmead ME20: Lark 6E **30**
W. Mill Rd. ME20: Lark 7E **30**
WEST MINSTER 4A **52**
Westminster Sq.
ME16: Maid 7E **36**
Westmorland Cl. ME15: Maid 5D **44**
Westmorland Grn.
ME15: Maid 5D **44**
Westmorland Rd.
ME15: Maid 5D **44**
W. Motney Way ME8: Rain 5F **17**
Westmount Av.
ME4: Chat'm 5B **4** (4D **14**)
Weston Rd. ME2: Strood 1J **13**
West Pk. Rd. ME15: Maid 2A **44**
West Pas. *ME12: S'ness 1A 52*
(off Charles St.)
ME12: S'ness 2A 52
(off West La.)
Westree Ct.
ME16: Maid 5F **7** (1H **43**)
Westree Rd.
ME16: Maid 5F **7** (1H **43**)
West Ridge ME10: Sit 4B **28**
West Rd. ME4: Chat'm 1E **14**
West St. ME2: Strood 6K **9**
ME7: Gill 3J **5** (2H **15**)
ME10: Sit 3C **28**
ME12: S'ness 2A **52**
ME15: Hunt 6A **48**
ME17: H'shm 6K **47**
ME19: W Mal 3C **34**
Westview ME4: St Mary 5F **11**
West Vw. Cotts.
ME17: Cha S 3H **51**
West Wlk. ME16: Maid 1E **42**
Westway ME17: Cox 2F **49**
Westwood Rd. ME15: Maid 5K **43**
Westwood Wlk. ME9: N'tn 2D **24**
Wet End Rd. ME20: Lark 7E **30**
Wetheral Dr. ME5: W'slade 5F **21**
Wexford Pl. ME15: Maid 6C **44**
Weybridge Cl.
ME5: Lord W 5G **21**
Wey Cl. ME5: Lord W 4G **21**
Weyhill Cl. ME14: Maid 5B **38**
Weymouth Rd. ME3: Wain 4B **10**
Wharf, The ME4: Chat'm 6E **10**
Wharfdale Sq. ME15: Maid 3H **43**
Wharf Rd. ME7: Gill 1H **5** (1G **15**)
(not continuous)
ME15: Maid 2H **43**
Wharf Way ME10: Sit 2D **28**
Whatman Cl. ME14: Maid 5B **38**
Wheatcroft Cl. ME10: Sit 3F **29**
Wheatcroft Gro. ME8: Gill 2F **23**
Wheatear Way ME5: W'slade 2F **21**
Wheatfield ME19: Leyb 2F **35**
Wheatfields ME5: Lord W 7H **21**
ME14: Weav 7C **38**
Wheatsheaf All.
ME12: S'ness 2C 52
(off High St.)
Wheatsheaf Cl. ME15: Maid 4A **44**
Wheatsheaf Gdns.
ME12: S'ness 3B **52**
Wheeler Pl. ME19: Kings H 2B **40**
Wheelers, The ME8: Wigm 3B **22**
Wheeler's La. ME17: Lint 5G **49**
Wheeler St.
ME14: Maid 2K **7** (6K **37**)
Wheeler St. Hedges
ME14: Maid, Pen H 5A **38**
(not continuous)
Wheelwrights, The
ME17: H'shm 6K **47**
Whetynton Cl.
ME2: Med E 2A **4** (2C **14**)
Whiffen's Av.
ME4: Chat'm 3C **4** (3D **14**)
Whiffen's Av. W.
ME4: Chat'm 3C **4** (3D **14**)
Whiffen Wlk. ME19: E Mal 2J **35**
Whimbrel Cl. ME10: Sit 6D **26**
Whimbrel Grn. ME20: Lark 1G **35**
Whimbrels, The
ME4: St Mary 6F **11**
Whimbrel Wlk. ME5: Lord W 1G **33**
Whitchurch Cl. ME16: Maid 7H **37**
Whitcombe Cl. ME5: Lord W 7G **21**
White Admiral Gro.
ME9: Iwade 2B **26**
Whitebeam Dr. ME17: Cox 2E **48**
White Cotts. ME14: S'lng 2H **37**
Whitedyke Rd.
ME6: Hall'g, Snod 7A **18**
White Ga. ME2: Strood 6H **9**
Whitegate Ct. *ME8: Parkw 4D 22*
(off Campleshon Rd.)
Whitehall Ct. ME10: Sit 5D **28**
Whitehall Rd. ME10: Sit 5C **28**
White Hart M. ME10: Sit 1C **28**
Whitehead Dr. ME2: Strood 4G **13**
Whiteheads La. ME14: Bear 7G **39**
White Hill Rd. ME14: Det 7D **22**
Whitehorse Hill ME5: Chat'm 5F **15**
White Horse La.
ME15: Otham 6F **45**
White Horse Stone 5C **32**
White Horse Wood Country Pk.
2J **39**
White Ho. Cl. ME3: Hoo W 3J **11**
Whitehouse Cres. ME1: Burh 2J **31**
White Leaves Ri. ME2: Cux 5D **12**
Whitepost Wood La.
ME20: Aylfd 4C **36**
White Rd.
ME4: Chat'm 7D **4** (7E **14**)
White Rock Ct. ME16: Maid 1H **43**
White Rock Pl.
ME16: Maid 5F **7** (1H **43**)
Whitewall Cen. ME2: Med E 7B **10**
Whitewall Rd.
ME2: Med E 1D **6** (7B **10**)
Whitewall Way
ME2: Med E 1E **6** (1B **14**)
Whitmore St. ME16: Maid 2F **43**
Whittaker St.
ME4: Chat'm 5D **4** (4E **14**)
Whornes Pl. ME2: Cux 7D **12**
Whybornes Chase
ME12: Minst 5J **53**
Whyman Av. ME4: Chat'm 7E **14**
Wicken Ho.
ME16: Maid 3F **7** (7H **37**)
Wickens Pl. ME19: W Mal 3D **34**
Wickham Cl. ME9: N'tn 3D **24**
Wickham St. ME1: Roch 5B **14**
Wickham Ter. *ME11: Queen 7A 52*
(off North Rd.)
Widgeon Rd. ME2: Strood 2F **13**
WIERTON 5D **50**
Wierton Hill ME17: Bou Mo 7C **50**
Wierton Rd. ME17: Bou Mo 3D **50**
Wigeon Rd. ME9: Iwade 3C **26**
WIGMORE 5B **22**
Wigmore Glade ME8: Wigm 5B **22**
Wigmore Rd. ME8: Wigm 5B **22**
(not continuous)
Wihtred Rd. ME9: Bap 5H **29**
Wilberforce Rd. ME17: Cox 2G **49**
Wildfell Cl. ME5: W'slade 2F **33**
Wildman Cl. ME8: Parkw 6D **22**
Wildwood Glade ME7: Hpstd 5B **22**
Wiley Ho. *ME7: Gill 3G 5*
(off Mill Rd.)
Wilkinson Pl. ME19: Kings H 2B **40**
Wilks Cl. ME8: Rain 6H **17**
Will Adams Ct.
ME7: Gill 3H **5** (2G **15**)
Will Adams Memorial 6J **15**
WILL ADAMS NHS TREATMENT CENTRE 4A **16**
Will Adams Rdbt. ME8: Gill 6K **15**
Will Adams Way ME8: Gill 7K **15**
William Baker Ho.
ME20: Aylfd 3C **36**
William Rigby Dr.
ME12: Minst 5E **52**
William Rd. ME2: Cux 6E **12**
William St. ME8: Rain 6G **17**
ME10: Sit 4C **28**
WILLINGTON 4D **44**
Willington Grn. ME15: Maid 5D **44**
Willington St. ME15: Maid 1E **44**
Willington Street (Maidstone) (Park & Ride) 1E **44**
Willis Cotts. ME7: B'hst 2K **33**
Willis Ct. ME12: Minst 7F **53**
Willis Ho. ME1: Roch 7C **6**
Willow Av. ME3: Hoo W 4J **11**
Willowbank Ct. ME15: Maid 4K **7**
Willowbrook Pl. *ME15: Maid 3K 43*
(off Regent Cl.)
Willowby Gdns. ME8: Parkw 5E **22**
Willow Cott. ME2: Hall'g 3C **18**
Willow Ct. ME15: Maid 6K **43**
Willow Grange ME3: Hoo W 2H **11**
Willowherb Cl.
ME4: St Mary 6G **11**
Willow Ho. ME5: W'slade 5D **20**
ME10: Sit 4F **29**
ME12: S'ness 2B 52
(off Hope St.)
ME16: Barm 1D **42**
Willow Industries
ME14: S'lng 7D **32**
Willowmead ME19: Leyb 1F **35**
Willow Ri. ME15: Bear 3E **44**
Willow Rd. ME2: Strood 2G **13**
ME20: Lark 7B **30**
Willows, The ME5: W'slade 1D **32**
ME8: Rain 6E **16**
ME9: N'tn 3D **24**
ME10: Kems'y 5D **26**
ME12: Minst 3H **53**
Willowside ME6: Snod 1C **30**
Willow Trees ME8: Wigm 3B **22**
Willow Way ME15: Maid 1A **44**
Willow Wood ME15: Maid 7D **44**
Wilmecote Ct. ME8: Gill 1D **22**
Wilmington Way ME8: Gill 6B **16**
Wilson Av. ME1: Roch 7B **14**
Wilson Cl. ME15: Maid 5D **44**
Wilsonian Sailing Club 4G **11**
Wilsons La. ME15: E Far 1D **48**
Wilton Dr. ME20: Dit 3J **35**
Wilton Ter. ME10: Sit 4K **25**
Wiltshire Cl. ME5: Chat'm 1G **21**
Wiltshire Way ME15: Maid 4D **44**
Wimbourne Dr. ME8: Gill 3D **22**
Winchelsea Rd.
ME5: W'slade 3F **21**
Winchester Av. ME5: W'slade 5D **20**
Winchester Ho. ME15: Maid 5C **44**
Winchester Pl.
ME14: Maid 1K **7** (6K **37**)
Winchester Way ME8: Rain 7G **17**
Windermere Dr. ME8: Gill 2D **22**
Windermere Gro. ME10: Sit 4B **28**
Windermere Ho. ME15: Maid 5C **44**
Windmill Cl. ME2: Strood 6K **9**
Windmill Ct. *ME12: S'ness 2C 52*
(off Broadway)
ME17: Bou Mo 2A **50**
Windmill Hgts. ME14: Bear 7G **39**
Windmill La. Caravan Site
ME19: W Mal 6B **34**
Windmill La. E. ME19: W Mal 5C **34**
Windmill La. W.
ME19: W Mal 6C **34**
Windmill Mnr. ME7: Gill 7H **5**
Windmill Rd. ME7: Gill 7G **5** (5F **15**)
(not continuous)
ME10: Sit 1B **28**
Windmill St. ME2: Strood 6K **9**
Windsock Rd. ME5: Chat'm 3B **20**
Windsor Av. ME4: Chat'm 6D **14**
Windsor Cl. ME14: Maid 5A **38**
Windsor Ct. ME7: Gill 4K **5** (3H **15**)
Windsor Dr. ME10: Sit 5B **28**
Windsor Rd.
ME7: Gill 4K **5** (3H **15**)
ME19: Kings H 7E **34**
Windward Rd. ME1: Roch 7A **14**
Windyridge ME7: Gill 7J **15**
Winford M. ME1: Roch 6J **13**
Wingate Ct. *ME10: Sit 3C 28*
(off Anselm Cl.)
Wingham Cl. ME8: Gill 5C **16**
ME15: Maid 5E **44**
Wingrove Dr.
ME2: Strood 1C **6** (7A **10**)
ME14: Weav 6D **38**
Winifred Rd. ME15: Bear 1E **44**
Winstanley Rd. ME12: S'ness 2C **52**
Winston Av. ME19: Kings H 1C **40**
Winston Dr. ME2: Wain 5B **10**
Winston Rd. ME2: Strood 3F **13**
Winterfield La. ME19: W Mal 3F **35**
Wintergreen Cl.
ME4: St Mary 6G **11**
Wirrals, The ME5: W'slade 5E **20**
WISDOM HOSPICE 6B **14**
Wises La. ME9: B'den 6J **25**
ME10: Sit 4J **25**
Witham Way ME2: Strood 1H **13**
Wittersham Cl.
ME5: W'slade 4F **21**
Wivenhoe Cl. ME8: Rain 6G **17**
Wodehouse Cl. ME20: Lark 6B **30**
Wolfe Ho. ME4: Chat'm 7F **11**
Wolfe Rd. ME16: Maid 2E **42**
Wollaston Cl. ME8: Parkw 6D **22**
Woodberry Dr. ME10: Sit 4F **29**
Woodbridge Dr. ME15: Maid 3H **43**
Woodbury Rd. ME5: W'slade 1D **32**
Woodchurch Cl. ME5: W'slade 4F **21**
Woodchurch Cres. ME8: Gill 6C **16**
Woodchurch Ho. ME8: Gill 6C **16**
Wood Cl. ME20: Aylfd 3B **36**
Wood Ct. *ME12: S'ness 2C 52*
(off Wood St.)
ME16: Barm 2D **42**
Woodcourt Cl. ME10: Sit 5C **28**
Woodcut ME14: Pen H 3K **37**
Woodcut Cotts. ME17: Holl 1A **46**
Woodfield Way
ME3: C'den, Wain 3B **10**
Woodford Gro.
ME19: Kings H 1C **40**
Woodford Rd. ME16: Maid 2E **42**

SAFETY CAMERA INFORMATION

PocketGPSWorld.com's CamerAlert is a self-contained speed and red light camera warning system for SatNavs and Android or Apple iOS smartphones/tablets. Visit www.cameralert.co.uk to download.

Safety camera locations are publicised by the Safer Roads Partnership which operates them in order to encourage drivers to comply with speed limits at these sites. It is the driver's absolute responsibility to be aware of and to adhere to speed limits at all times.

By showing this safety camera information it is the intention of Geographers' A-Z Map Company Ltd., to encourage safe driving and greater awareness of speed limits and vehicle speed. Data accurate at time of printing.

Printed and bound in the United Kingdom by Gemini Press Ltd., Shoreham-by-Sea, West Sussex
Printed on materials from a sustainable source